Great American Brewpubs and Gastropubs

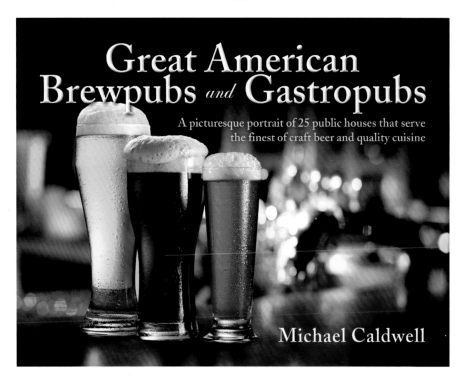

A picturesque portrait of 25 public houses that serve
the finest of beer and quality cuisine

Michael Caldwell

Great American Brewpubs and Gastropubs

ISBN: 978-0-9784620-6-2

Cover and Book Design by Chris Mendoza

Front Cover Photograph: Shutterstock

Printed in Korea by the Four Colour Print Group

Great American Brewpubs and Gastropubs

Introduction

The United Kingdom has long been the source of inspiration for the world's most beloved "tavern" or "pub"; providing residents with their own community public house for social interaction, hearty brews and libations, and traditional "pub grub"- a winning combination, regardless of the continent, or city. No stranger to the concept or value of a public house, two distinct styles of artisan pubs have separated themselves from the packs, and grabbed the heart strings of Americans - the enduring micro brewpub, and the delicious new gastropub.

Microbrewery pub house owners, and their employees, are a special lot of people, who are wholly committed to hard work the old fashioned way, and quality in everything they serve. A microbrewery is defined as a beer production facility that produces a limited amount of craft beer, ranging from 2 to 20 bbls *(a brewer's barrel)*, with a production size of less than 15,000 barrels of beer annually. These small scale craft microbreweries are independently owned and operated, with traditional experimentation and operations reflecting the spirit of Old World European beer production dating back to Trappist monks some 2,000 years ago. As of 2012, the American Brewers Association reported 2,075 craft breweries in North America, with just 1,195 of those operating as brewpubs. Brewpubs not only handcraft their own unique lines of beers and sodas, but provide their communities with a pub house, where they serve them fresh from the tap, accompanied by food.

Unlike many restaurants, brewpubs create the beers they serve on-premise, while sustaining the farms in their community by sourcing wheat, grain, barley and malts, locally. Their food offering is most often of the highest caliber, as most brewpubs send their spent grains back to local farms to feed livestock, resulting in healthier poultry, pork and beef, which they in turn use in the creation of their pub fare. House beer braised meats and dishes, made-from-scratch pizza dough, and gourmet grain-fed burgers served on fresh homemade buns, are among the high-quality pub fare that accompanies the brewpubs' one-of-a-kind ales, lagers, stouts and Root Bier. Some of the featured "best of the best" brewpubs have histories dating back before the notorious Prohibition Era *(between 1920 and 1933)*, adding another layer of endurance and staying power to these hidden treasures within our communities. Other brewpubs are the first of their kind within their respective communities, and embraced all the more for their matchless offering in handcrafted beers, made local, by locals, for locals.

While beers and spirits have always been the draw to the pub environment, and little emphasis placed on the pub grub of our past, this category of cuisine has had its staying power. Today, it's hard to find a British-inspired pub that doesn't offer patrons some variation of the traditional Shepherd's Pie, Fish & Chips, and Bangers & Mash, along with hearty stews and burgers. As a result of renewed global interest in healthier cuisine, and a recommitment to our farmers, orchard growers and creameries, the portmanteau of gastronomy and pub, now known as the "gastropub", was born. The incorporation of gastronomy into our pubs translates to our favorite bowls and platters, now made with quality ingredients, including organic and free-range poultry, grain-fed beef and pork, and fresh locally grown produce, along with artisan cheese and condiments. For the last decade, traditional pubs have been reinvigorated with the addition of classically trained chefs, and the creation of sophisticated and high-end food offerings to replace the aploughman's lunch from our past, elevating pubs to a whole new niche market for trendy and health conscious foodies everywhere. It didn't take long for this latest food trend from Clerkenwell, London, to make its way across the pond, with gastropubs springing up from forward-thinking restaurateurs in North America, from coast to coast.

Gastropub owners, and their employees, are a new brand of responsible restaurateurs who are wholly committed to serving quality food and libations, while maintaining the casual pub atmosphere we've all grown to cherish. They source the best, fresh, responsibly raised and grown ingredients, and in doing so, strengthen their communities by supporting the local producers of their region. Gastropub owners are equally committed to the beers, wines and spirits they serve, pairing their sophisticated cuisine with the best craft beers and boutique wines from their region, and across the globe, depending on their specific niche. Many also showcase private collections of our favorite timeless spirits, serving authentic Scottish Whiskey, Kentucky Bourbons, and specialty cocktails.

Great American Brewpubs and Gastropubs is a celebration of the most notable artisan public houses in North America, and the unique beers and food they handcraft and serve within their communities, to their neighbors, and friends. Each chapter has been designed with precise details and pictures to give readers a glimpse into these rare microbrewery and gastronomy operations, and includes special facts about their location, atmosphere, and the people they serve, many renowned as destination locations by tourists and locals alike. Each of the dedicated entrepreneurs is featured, along with the range and wealth of artisan libations they create, serve and share, as well as their gastronomic niche.

Whether you're a home brewer, connoisseur of cask-conditional ales, beer geek, grape lover, or Scotch, Sake or soda drinker, there's a special libation for each and every palate. Vegans, gluten-free diners, and aficionados of

pork belly, fresh mussels, and upscale dining in a sunny Beer Garden will not be disappointed. Warm yourself fireside at an authentic Canadian lodge, devour a gourmet burger in a beachside man cave, or simply belly up to the bar for a hearty one-of-a-kind Imperial Stout and Celtic music. Bring your appetite, no matter your taste, and savor the craft beers and quality cuisine of 25 of the great American brewpubs and gastropubs.

Table of Contents

THE PUB

The chic, family-owned and operated, 775 Gastropub is located on the Westside of the Meadowood Mall in Reno, Nevada, featuring high-end food and one of the largest selections of beers "from around the world" on the West coast. This gastropub is a decadent detour for shoppers from the "Food Court", and with a direct non-mall entrance of inviting awning and outdoor smoking patio with cozy sitting area - a great hide-away tavern, beer pub, singles mixer, and date restaurant. 775 Gastropub's European-trained Chef Auriane Ugalde uses fresh and local meats, dairy, produce and grains to turn ordinary "pub grub" into innovative bistro cuisine. The menu reflects a combination of time-honored pub favorites and upscale fine dining to delight every palate, and satisfy every wallet. Owners, John and Sarah Leniz pair their quality food with over 200 of the world's best crafted beers, a creative blend of 775 trademark infused liquors and handcrafted cocktails, and wines from California, Spain, Argentina, France, Germany, Italy and South Africa.

The friendly environment, casual dining atmosphere, and excellent quality beer, food and prices attract a diverse group of patrons, seven days a week. The 775 Gastropub hosts guests to comfortable lunch or dinner at the bar, family dinners, fun-filled nights out with friends, intimate and economical date nights, group events and parties. Special events at the 775 include 6-course paired Beer Dinners featuring a different guest brewery held every other month opposite their ever popular Massages & Martinis event. In addition to the house menu, 775 Gastropub features an unbeatable Sunday Brunch menu and through their "Charity of the Month" program donates a portion of all sales to local programs in support of their community.

OWNERS

John Leniz has worked as a restaurant and bar manager at various well-known locales in Reno for years. He and his wife, Sarah, operated a chain restaurant at the mall for two years, but knew they wanted to break out on their own. They saw an opportunity to provide higher quality food and beverage, in a relaxed, casual atmosphere. Both natives of northern Nevada, and community focused, the new owners revitalized the old restaurant with warm lighting, fresh décor, a new upscale menu, and a unique selection of beers and libations. The

WELCOME TO 775

EASE WAIT BE SEATED

Lenizs are both passionate about good food and good drinks, each adding their own nuances to this extraordinary tavern, with a warm family environment. They opened the doors to their 775 Gastropub guests, old and new, on May 12, 2010. John and Sarah Leniz live full time in Reno, with their three young children, and share in the operation of their family business, where "Our place is your place."

ATMOSPHERE

The 775 Gastropub provides indoor table seating in a comfortable masculine pub atmosphere, and features a quaint patio with wooden picnic tables for outdoor dining and drinks. The horseshoe mahogany bar provides seating for twenty with swivel high-back bar stools, generous counter space for eating, and plenty of elbow room. There is a cozy recreation area where patrons enjoy friendly games of billiards and darts. Chess and checker boards are always available, along with puzzles and games for younger diners. Wall-mounted televisions featuring college and professional football, racing, baseball, and seasonal favorites provide tavern entertainment, along with local musicians on special nights. The Lenizs also feature an eclectic art collection of "old downtown" Reno throughout the gastropub including a twenty foot wall mural. The mural pays tribute to the first Reno arch erected to commemorate the completion of the transcontinental highway. The city later held a contest in search of a slogan to adorn the arch. "The Biggest Little City in the World" was the winner, awarding a grand prize of $100!

Beer and Spirits

The 775 Gastropub offers beer connoisseurs one of the most incredible selection of beers, highlighting diverse flavors on tap, in bottles and in cans. The 775 bar features a rotating tap with 23 drafts attentively served in 8 to 20 ounce glassware to best highlight the aroma, color and flavor of each. Patrons savor a flute of aromatic Lindeman's Framboise, enjoy a decadent blend of pale ale and malt in a 16 ounce English pint of Young's Double Chocolate Stout Nitro, or make their way through a 13 ounce Unibroue Trois Pistoles, boasting flavors of cocoa, ripe fruit, and dark spices, finishing like an old port. American classics and international bottled beers provide a wide and far-reaching range, and include the Dogfish Head Chateau Jiahu, a beer recipe of

rice, honey, grape and hawthorn fruits dating back 9,000 years in China. Beer flights are a favorite option for new guests, while the Beer Club offers rewards for different achievements. Several guests have earned the status of "Beer Jedi", entitling them to lifetime discounts on all beers. Beer Dinners feature a gourmet dinner of six courses, each paired with a special beer from a guest brewery. 775 is proud to have played host to such breweries as Lagunitas, Deschutes, Rogue, Evil Twin, Mikkeller and Stone, just to name a few.

The 775 wine cellar is stocked with an eclectic variety of white, red, and rose wines sold by the glass, or bottle. The diverse range of wines features the grapes of California, Spain, Argentina, France, Germany, Italy and South Africa.

The 775 Gastropub also serves a wide range of cocktails and spirits, including handcrafted cocktails made from in-house infused liquors. The 775 Bloody Mary is made using vodka infused with sun dried tomatoes, lemons, peppercorns, fresh rosemary and basil. A tequila infused with habanera peppers adds extra punch to the 775's Macho Margarita, while the 775 Old Fashioned features bacon infused bourbon. Guests enjoy endless choices with a special libation for everyone, from Ultimate Chocolate Martinis to the Mimosa 775, made with fresh oj, squeezed right at the bar when you order it!

CUISINE

Gastropubs are traditional taverns that serve high quality beers, wines and spirits, accompanied by great quality food. 775 Gastropub's Chef Auriane Ugalde features a diverse menu combining long-time pub favorites with a gourmet twist, and sophisticated lunch and dinner specials using seasonal, local and fresh ingredients.

The 775 Gastropub's trademark appetizer, the Blue Chip Deal, features hand-cut russet potato chips tossed in melted blue cheese, roast garlic and butter, topped with a balsamic reduction and green onions. It is one of the most popular dishes ordered for any occasion.

The 775 Gastropub is very pleased to offer it's patrons many different burger patty options including turkey, house made Basque chorizo, a veggie portabella cap, bison and venison. The all beef "775 Classic Burger" is the featured signature burger, featuring fresh ground, all grass fed beef from Alpine Ranch. The cattle roam freely over 800,000 acres, located 60 miles East of Fallon, Nevada, unconfined, foraging in the mountains and meadows. The "Nevada Raised Beef" contains no hormones, antibiotics, processed or packaged feed, grains nor animal bi-products. This beef is truly grass fed and NOT grain finished, highlighting the commitment of both the owners and the executive chef to supporting area farmers and providing local sourced meats for customers.

Once patrons choose their patty, they can dress it with any of 20 custom burger toppings,

ranging from oven roasted tomatoes, grilled sweet onions and manchego cheese, to pork belly and a fried egg!

The seasonal, chef driven menu offers a variety of delicious vegetarian, vegan and gluten-free dishes, fresh seafood, and a special Kid's Menu of PB&J, macaroni-and-cheese, chicken nuggets, sliders and corn dogs. 775 Gastropub is sure to have something to please patrons of all ages and palates. And with Weekly Chef's Specials offering nine new items each week, you could eat something different each day of the year! Desserts include the famous white and dark chocolate layered Tuxedo Cake, Lemon Raspberry Triffle, and Brownie Torte served with chocolate sauce and whipped cream. Sunday Brunches at the 775 include hot breakfast favorites prepared gourmet-style, such as the Sourdough Blueberry Pancakes served "in the pan" and Crème Brulee Stuffed French Toast, complimented by the "build your own" Bloody Mary bar.

775
GASTROPUB

BLUE STAR BREWERY

THE PUB

The Blue Star Brewing Company opened in 1996 and is located at the beginning of the Mission Reach, a major bike-friendly and pedestrian friendly thoroughfare to the city's cultural and historical features that runs along the San Antonio River.

This eclectic craft brewery and restaurant is a central watering hole and activity hub for locals and hundreds of thousands of visitors each year. The craft beer made on premise, and elevated pub food, are served six days a week using fresh and locally raised and grown ingredients. Owner, Joey Villarreal and his wife, Magdalena have fostered a strong bond with their community, elevating their classic pub dishes through their alliance with local farmers. The food is made with quality ingredients prepared simply. Blue Star Brewing Company's friendly neighborhood atmosphere is rivaled only by the quality food and beer it serves. Weekly live bands and entertainment, Spurs shuttle, late-night shows, group bike rides, and countless other community events have made this unique restaurant and brewery a destination location for locals and tourists, alike.

THE OWNER

Blue Star Brewing Company was founded by entrepreneur and restaurateur Joey Villarreal and his wife, Magdalena. Joey majored in biology at the University of Texas San Antonio where he first encountered home brewing. After college, he opened "Joey's" on North St. Mary's in 1988. It was during a trip to Cleveland, Ohio, in 1992 that the brewpub concept peaked Joey's interest. He visited the Great Lakes Brewing Company, at the time a 7-barrel brew house, and was drawn to the operation's "realness" and human ingenuity. He spent the next 4 years developing his own operation, what in 1996 came to fruition as the Blue Star Brewing Company. The mission: to serve house-made craft-brewed beer using wholesome ingredients.

Although Texas law prohibits self-distribution, limiting Texas brewpubs to on-site sales only, Joey continues to work to change the current beer law. The hope is to see the law changed with all it's restrictions lifted, thereby opening the beer market and facilitating the making and selling of Texas craft beer in Texas.

Joey's entrepreneurial spirit and attentiveness to

customer wants and needs led to the opening of Joe Blues, a full bar located across the parking lot from the brewery. In 2004, he opened the Blue Star Bike Shop located next door to the brewery to provide convenient fun transportation for exploring the historic San Antonio Missions Trail. The bike shop and the bar add even more appeal to the hopping Blue Star Brewing Company.

The Atmosphere

The Blue Star Brewing Company is situated at the river gateway to the city's natural, cultural and historical features, connecting the new and contemporary of the Blue Star Arts Complex and the rest of the city, with the old and historic of the Spanish missions. The riparian ecosystem provides as much entertainment as does the surrounding art galleries, retail stores, restaurants and bars for those who love to appreciate nature. The Blue Star Brewing Company is centrally located on South Alamo Street and is accessible by trolley and the San Antonio River. The Blue Star Brewing Company has continued to grow in popularity over the past two decades as a favorite watering hole for the large and lively community of local artists and residents. The brewery and restaurant are located in a large rustic warehouse building, regularly serving as the neighborhood's central hub for live entertainment, Spurs games,

late-night shows and a wide range of community events including a monthly art walk and group bike rides. Convenient cruiser-styled bike rentals and the large outdoor beer garden enrich the appeal of this casual pedestrian-friendly neighborhood tavern.

The Beer

Blue Star Brewing Company makes all of their beer in-house using organic ingredients. After two decades of experimentation and experience, Villarreal now sticks with a simple base of 2-3 yeast strains to produce most of his year-round varieties. BSBC patrons savor a wide array of hand-crafted stouts, lagers and ales from a rotating tap, including the seasonal favorite, King William Ale, a traditional barley wine-styled beer containing large quantities of malt and hops. While Texas laws have been slow to accommodate craft beer distribution, Blue Star enthusiasts can take their favorite craft beers home in 32 oz. medicine bottles, 64oz. stainless steel containers, and kegs.

The Menu

The Blue Star Brewing Company provides a fresh and well-sourced menu for lunch, dinner and Sunday brunch, featuring innovative comfort food, favorite pub classics, fresh-baked breads and desserts.

The Blue Star Burger is made with local, grass-fed beef and served with crisp, house-cut fries. The Butcher's Block, a variety of excellent cuts of meat changes daily, offering guests a new selection each time they visit. Among the various options vegetarians can enjoy are the Farmer's Market Vegetable Platter or the Mission Trail Mix Salad.

Aromatically enticing breads are baked fresh daily, including a rich brioche, baguettes and Ciabatta. Desserts offered include the Triple Chocolate Layer Cake, Bread Pudding with Whiskey Anglaise and house-made gelatos and ice cream. All are made with the same quality and care that distinguishes Blue Star Brewing

Company's menu as a whole.

The Villarreals partner with local farmers to purvey farm-raised beef, chicken, dairy, eggs, grains, fruits and vegetables to create delicious cuisine.

The Cambridge House Brew Pub

The Pub

The Cambridge House Brew Pub, located at 357 Salmon Brook Street in the heart of Granby, Connecticut, is a family-style tavern and microbrewery in one, serving patrons real craft beers, food and live entertainment. The microbrewery has produced 100 separate beers over the past seven years, with award-winning originals, including Three Steve Stout, Alt 45, Ominous Forecast, Copper Hill Kolsch and its renowned Abijah Rowe IPA. Owner Scott Riley pairs these craft beers with a food menu of classic pub fare, including American grilled burgers and steaks, and inventive comfort food for every palate, followed by two distinct signature desserts. CBH procures fresh ingredients for their food and libations, supporting the local farms and farmers of Connecticut and Massachusetts.

This lively neighborhood brew pub hosts locals, guests and 200 Mug Club members to lunch and dinner six days a week, and features live music, beer dinners, tastings and pub crawls on the weekend.

Owner

Scott worked as a chemical engineer and environmental manager before trying his hand in the restaurant business. With an entrepreneurial spirit and a true affinity for home brewing, craft beer and real food, he spent years evaluating brew pubs, taverns and other establishments while planning his move. When he came across the opportunity to buy the Cambridge House Brew Pub, he knew he was home. With the support of his wife and the community of Granby, the brewery and pub were purchased in October 2009. The challenge was set to retain what made the pub initially successful and rebuild the business. Riley recognized that the loyal patrons deserved the best beer and food that could be provided, and The Cambridge House Brew Pub re-launch was met with enthusiasm and renewed hope. The Cambridge House continues to maintain itself as a family place where everyone knows everyone, a favorite watering hole for locals and travelers alike, the kind of establishment that brings people and communities together during tough times for good times. Riley and his team hold true to the new brew pub motto – "Real Beer, Real Food, Real People".

ATMOSPHERE

How do you manage to project an aura of class, while being an inviting, fun place for family, friends, and individuals? The Cambridge House does it with the look of a classic New England brewpub, combining style with a welcoming atmosphere. Hang around at the bar of this large residential-style building, watching sports on one of the many TV's, or even watching the brewer through the windows into the microbrewery. Or maybe you want to be in the bar area but have a little more quiet – try the spacious dining room, or even the outdoor patio with a friendly ambiance all its own. Or rise above it all in the elegantly decorated upstairs dining room, providing a private setting for wedding receptions, showers, birthday parties, banquets and other special events when not in use for regular dining. So whether its casual lunches and dinners paired with its handcrafted brews, a quick pint on the way home from work, or a late night rocking to the open mic and local bands, The Cambridge House is the spot.

BEER AND SPIRITS

With five serving tank beer lines and seven keg beer lines, The Cambridge House Brew Pub features a rotating menu of its hand crafted beers along with selected guest taps. Once in a while,

they will put twelve of their beers on tap for a real special occasion, providing beer connoisseurs with a rich journey, sipping their way from the light lagers, through pale ales out to the hearty stouts. New patrons often start with the sampler paddle, which can accommodate up to five beers. This microbrewery has produced 100 brew varieties using a traditional brewing process of: mashing, sparging, boiling, fermenting and conditioning. Award winning favorites include the Copper Hill Kolsch *(a smooth German-style light ale with noble hop character)*, the Abijah Rowe IPA *(a traditional English India Pale Ale brewed with English malt and a blend of English and American hops)*, and the bicuityycrisp ESB

(a traditional English medium-bodied ale made with noble hops). The rich Bumble Bock, a Pigskin Brown of toffee, golden raisins and coffee undertones, and the Bourbon barrel-aged Imperial Moonbeam Stout are among the recent special features. Cambridge House craft beers are poured fresh from the tap into pint glasses, or for the mug club, official numbered 20-ounce English dimpled glass mugs. Tastings, pub crawls, beer dinners, community events, and Mug Club parties provide Cambridge House regulars and the 200 Mug Club members with endless recreation and fun. The Cambridge House Brew Pub also operates a full liquor bar for spirits drinkers, and provides its grape

drinkers with an evolving selection of local and international wines.

Cuisine

The Cambridge House has a large food menu of classic pub meals, often incorporating their crafted beers into their marinades, sauces and dishes. Riley and his culinary team procure a lot of fresh, local ingredients for their menu, elevating the food they serve, while supporting local farmers of the area. Diners enjoy savory starters of stout marinated steak skewers, fried calamari, quesadillas, CBH wings made with a variety of sauces and dry rubs, loaded pub nachos, homemade chili and more.

The menu includes a variety of chicken or seafood pastas and salads, gourmet burgers, sandwiches and wraps, along with flame grilled pizzas, and hearty pub dinner entrees. Dinner favorites include the house Mac & Cheese,

meatloaf covered in stout mushroom gravy, beer-battered fish and chips, a 12 ounce house rib-eye, and tender St. Louis pork ribs. Burgers and sandwiches are served with brew pub fries, sweet potato fries, or beer-battered onion rings.

Two signature desserts are available - a decadent Chocolate Brownie Sundae and *(a spicy version called)* the Aztec Brownie Sundae. The homemade brownies infuse Young's Double Chocolate Stout in the batter and are served with local ice cream. The Gran-Val Scoop in Granville, Ma makes the ice creams and mixes cayenne in the chocolate ice cream for the CBH Aztec Brownie, giving this favorite dessert its extra tickle!

DATZ

THE PUB

In South Tampa, Datz has carved itself a cozy niche in the lore of foodie legend. This is a serious eatery with quirky style and it's elevated comfort food to new heights by obsessing over the little details that can make or break a dish. The ingredients are seasonal and fresh, and the approach – always original. It's this dedication to making each plate special that has created what can only be described as a cult following. The gastropub regularly updates its menu and libations, and that effort to stay current truly sets Datz apart, as does its atmosphere. Its warm neighborhood vibe and eclectic menu makes everyone feel welcome, from vegetarians and seafood lovers to carnivores and chocolate fanatics, with a perfect accompaniment for beer lovers, wine connoisseurs, and boutique spirit drinkers. Owners Roger and Suzanne Perry serve up new culinary experiences seven days a week - serving breakfast, lunch, dinner, weekend brunch, and catered events. The Perrys also offer their patrons an opportunity to take a little bit of the Datz magic with them, by way of a gourmet shop on the ground floor of the restaurant that's stocked with thoughtfully selected local products. With so much to offer, it's no mystery why visiting dignitaries and celebrities line up next to local devotees to dine at Datz.

OWNERS

Roger Perry's tastes for fresh, seasonal foods started early. Raised on a working farm in Ohio, he grew up eating freshly laid eggs, farm-raised beef and pork, and fish caught and served fresh – all regular staples on his family supper table. After leaving the farm and graduating from Ohio State University, Roger purchased a small pet food company in Columbus, and grew it into the largest chain of pet food superstores in the Midwest. Over the years, Roger traveled across the country and to far flung locales in Brazil, Italy, and France on business ventures, discovering new flavors and cuisines. These adventures renewed his passion for quality food and in 2006, when he and Suzanne relocated from Ocala to Tampa, they decided to it was time to share their love of good eats. On January 28, 2009, the dynamic duo opened Datz and it quickly became an everyday oasis for their new community, putting crave-worthy food within reach.

Suzanne Perry has a long-held passion for giving back to the community and that's always been

evident in her professional endeavors. As co-owner of Datz, Suzanne manages many of the operations, including the marketing and PR components of the business. Under her leadership, Datz has supported a wealth of local charitable organizations, including The Junior League of Tampa, the American Heart Association, the Wounded Warrior Foundation, the Care Coalition, Tampa General Hospital, the St. Joseph's hospitals, University of South Florida, Hyde Park Preservation Inc., the Tampa Museum of Art, The Humane Society, and the Glazer Children's Museum. To her, giving back is a natural move for Datz; the place has an undeniable kinship with all things local.

"Datz is all about good food and good service in a unique, one-of-a-kind atmosphere. Giving back to the community is part of our 'localness' and core culture."

ATMOSPHERE

Datz is an upscale neighborhood gastropub and market in one, located in a spacious 8,000-square-foot building in South Tampa, just fifteen minutes from the airport. The interior design combines classic and modern elements for a charmingly funky result that is fun, warm, and welcoming. With every seat seemingly nestled into a quaint, cozy space, Datz nails the gastropub feel. The restaurant's

160 seats are dispersed between the upstairs Loft Bar and dining room, the inviting Tap Room Bar and casual market space downstairs, and an outdoor covered patio complete with misters and fans for hot Florida days. The Tap Room is the best place to cozy up to the bar and sample the dozens of craft beers on tap, including those from local, small-batch breweries. At the Loft Bar, Datz's artfully stocked wine collection is within arm's reach and by-the-glass vintages are poured from the cuvenee.

The Market showcases a wide range of gourmet, artisanal foods capable of appeasing even the most discriminating gourmand, and true to form, many of the products are of local origin. The shelves are stacked high with noteworthy delights – chocolates, fruit preserves, pasta, organic grits and nut butter, aged balsamic vinegar, and olive oil just to name a few.

Beer and Spirits
The beer and wine lists at Datz are distinctly American, a nod from the Perrys to the American farmers, vineyard owners, and brewers, who have created the perfect pairings for the American comfort food Datz serves. The menu features a respectable rotation of 34 beers on tap and the restaurant goes out of its way to feature limited edition and seasonal brews. Datz also stocks a small assortment of high-end and rare vintage bottled beers for true beer aficionados. If all that choice makes it hard to commit, ask the bartender to pour a flight and sample several.

Wine connoisseurs can take their pick from a large selection of carefully sourced wines served by the glass. Currently, the wine list showcases vineyards in California, Oregon and Washington with an impressive collection of great American bruts, blancs, Rieslings, chardonnays, pinot noirs, zinfandels, merlots and cabernets. The Datz global cellar offers a quality selection of international vintages from Argentina, Australia, Chile, France, Germany, South Africa, and Spain.

The full bar serves a colorful spirits menu of infused liquors, specialty house drinks, aged cocktails, and all of the classics, including

bourbon and scotch. The menu has something for every taste; on-trend savory apple-sage coolers, spicy made-to-order margaritas with jalapeno infused tequila, and creamy chocolate martinis are just the beginning.

Cuisine

The menu at Datz changes with the seasons and trends, providing new culinary adventures for every meal of every day. The back of the house has made an art of tweaking classics enough that they are fresh and interesting, but not so much that they are unrecognizable.

For breakfast the menu offers everything you'd find at your favorite diners from coast to coast, and then some: Southwestern Eggs Barbacoa, hearty Datz Hash, Brie Bardot sandwiches, Red Velvet Pancakes, and hot cinnamon Monkey Bread are all customer favorites. A special brunch menu is served all day Saturday and Sunday, combining decadent breakfast entrees with inventive salads, homemade soups, gourmet

burgers, and incredible sandwiches piled high with premium meats and cheeses.

Lunch at Datz can mean Honeyed Salmon on rice, the decadent Waffles n' Tweet, or an unbeatable 100% beef Mesquite Burger on a sweet sourdough bun with blue cheese drizzled, house made, sweet-n-salty potato chips. The sandwich menu alone offers an impressively wide array of options. Fill a fresh roll with savory, pan-seared meatloaf, corned beef, pulled pork, or house-smoked beef brisket, and your choice or tasty toppings. Appetizers, aptly titled "Splurges" on the Datz menu, include indulgent starters like homemade Mac n' Cheese Bites, Black Truffle Fries, Figtastic Flatbread *(flatbread topped with figs, Asian pear, roasted red onions, crumbly blue cheese, and arugula)*, and more.

Datz dinner headliners include mouth-watering meats, seafood, pastas, salads and vegetarian fare. Live high on the hog with the Korean Ribeye *(16 oz. marinated in hoisin/Coca-Cola glaze)* or keep it casual with Creole Shrimp & Grits or Fish n' Crisps. Naturally, all are served with a healthy helping of Datz's unique take on American culinary classics.

DIAMOND KNOT BREWERY AND ALEHOUSE

Diamond Knot
CRAFT BREWING

THE PUB

Diamond Knot Brewery is the first microbrewery in Mukilteo, Washington, and a leading producer of NW handcrafted beers serving the Puget Sound region, with distribution of Diamond Knot crafted bottled beers in 12 states, and draft beers in three, plus British Columbia. Owner Bob Maphet runs two breweries - B1 at the original Front Street location, and B2 at Chennault Beach Road, handcrafting 20 beer varieties each year, and producing up to 800 cases of beer per day. The Brewery & Alehouse, opened in 1999, sits in front of the original brewery, serving 12 handcrafted beers on tap along with traditional pub fare, in a warm and spirited atmosphere. The Diamond Knot Brewery & Alehouse is only 15 miles north of Seattle, and a destination location catering to locals of the Puget Sound, Boeing employees,

and tourists of the neighboring Mukilteo Lighthouse Park and Whidbey Island. The pub's creed is to provide patrons with exceptional craft beers, food and lively experiences. The unique Stonegrill concept, a hopping jukebox, and a National Trivia Network *(NTN)* provides up to 100 guests with interactive tavern fun with DK staff and other pub patrons.

OWNERS

Diamond Knot Craft Brewing was co-founded in 1994 by partners Bob Maphet and the late Brian Sollenberger. Both men worked for Boeing, where they met at the company's beer and wine club. Maphet and Sollenberger discovered their shared passion for craft beers, and began home brewing together. They started their original microbrewery in 300 square feet behind the former Cheers Too! pub on Front Street in 1994. In 1999, the Cheers Too! pub became the Diamond Knot Brewery & Alehouse, giving Diamond Knot beer patrons a place to enjoy their favorite brews onsite.

With the demand for craft beer increasing and a desire to expand the varieties of Diamond Knot craft beer, Maphet and Sollenberger hired Chief Fermentation Officer Pat Ringe. Then in 2002, the partners hired restaurateur, Andy Eason, to help with the Alehouse. Maphet and Sollenberger soon realized the magic of pairing their specially craft brews with specially crafted food, and a warm, lively environment for patrons to call their own again. By 2005, the original Diamond Knot Brewery could no longer fill all of the new demand for its beer, so a second

brewery and large-scale production facility was opened at Chennault Beach Road, Suite B2. As Diamond Knot beer rose in popularity, the partners opened two more pubs, one on Camano Island in 2007, and a Pizza House in Lincoln Courtyard in 2008. Sollenberger passed unexpectedly in 2009, and today, Maphet continues the Diamond Knot legacy, employing 75 employees to run two breweries, three pubs, and craft beer distribution throughout the Pacific NW, U.S. and British Columbia.

ATMOSPHERE

The Diamond Knot Brewery & Alehouse is located at 621 Front Street in "Old Town"

Mukilteo, adjacent to the waterfront and Mukilteo ferry terminal. This original alehouse has been a waterfront pub-house at the wharf for the past 30 years, reopened in 1999 under the Diamond Knot brand. The building itself is also historic, originally a bus garage for Mukilteo-Everett Stage, a local transit company that ran a bus route to Everett. The original roll up bay door, unique arched roof, exposed wooden roof trusses, and open plank ceiling provides patrons with an open yet rustic tavern atmosphere to celebrate this local business, and the handcrafted beers and food it provides. The Diamond Knot brewing process can be viewed through a large glass window separating the alehouse from the

original on-premise microbrewery, B1, in back.

BEER AND SPIRITS

Diamond Knot Craft Brewing produces 20 crafted beer varieties throughout the year at the B1 and B2 breweries. Diamond Knot crafted beers include a diverse and wide range of flavors in: Brown Ale, English Bitter, Golden Ale, Winter Ale, Hefeweizen, India Pale Ale, Vienna Ale, Imperial IPA, Barley Wine, American Porter, and Irish Dry Stout. The Diamond Knot Brewery & Alehouse serves 12-14 rotating craft beers on tap for pub patrons to sample, or savor in half pot, pint pot, pitchers, or kegs to-go. Maphet and Sollenberger were early pioneers of the historical India Pale Ale or IPA, the DK Craft Brewing's flagship beer made with Columbus hops, grapefruit and a hint of cedar, and a favorite with customers throughout North America.

Diamond Knot Brewery & Alehouse showcases a special cask-conditioned beer every Thursday night, providing patrons with a unique tasting of old-world flavors. DK brewers add a small amount of actively fermenting yeast to a keg of finished beer, creating a secondary-fermentation. Resulting brews are smooth and include dynamic concoctions like Peach-Ginger Golden Ale, Apple-Cinnamon ESB and Oaked IPA.

Diamond Knot Brewery & Alehouse also serves a small, well-sourced menu of local Washington State red and white wines for its grape drinkers. Columbia Valley is the largest wine region in Washington, encompassing 99% of the vineyards. The unique climate of the Columbia Valley produces fruit-forward wines, with the balance and structure of a European wine. Premium glasses or bottles are served of Chardonnay from Washington Hills and Pine & Post. Sagelands reds include a balanced black cherry and cedar Cabernet, and a ripe cherry, vanilla, oak Merlot.

CUISINE

The Diamond Knot Brewery & Alehouse provides guests with a large food menu of traditional pub fare, serving hearty starters of warm artichoke and crab dip, stuffed portabellas, a pound of house wings, layered nachos, loaded potato wheels, a homemade beer brat potato soup, fresh seafood chowder of smoked Pacific salmon, crab legs and clams, and lighter fare of inventive salads. Special house entrees feature stone-grilled steaks, salmon, prawns, hand-tossed pizzas, and gourmet sandwiches, both hot and cold.

The Australian Stonegrill System creates a unique cooking and serving experience for customers of the Diamond Knot Brewery & Alehouse. Flat non-porous salt slabs are used in place of traditional pans, reaching a prime cooking temperature of 725 degrees Fahrenheit in the oven. Entrees are served on the piping hot stones, designed to retain their heat throughout the meal. Stone-grilled steaks and entrees are the Diamond Knot headliners, featuring full pound cuts of T-bone, rib-eye and top sirloin marinated in a special house marinade overnight, and served with seasonal vegetables, baked potatoes, dinner rolls, steak sauce and creamy garlic horseradish. Fresh black tiger prawns, salmon steaks, fajitas and a slow cooked beef brisket are other stone-grilled menu favorites.

Homemade, hand-tossed, stone-grilled pizzas are also a big hit with pub patrons. Diners savor 15 flavorful pizzas from traditional to Thai Chicken, enjoying hot sausage, deli pastrami, pulled pork, Cajun crab, roasted vegetables and loads of fresh mozzarella on a crispy crust.

The Diamond Knot Brewery & Alehouse offers a small, but decadent dessert menu for patrons with a sweet tooth. The Chocolate Lovin' Spoonful Cake features three layers of dark, moist chocolate served with pools of chocolate sauce, whipped crème and chocolate chips. Diners also savor generous slices of Ultimate Cheesecake and Caramel Apple Crisp.

Diamond Knot
CRAFT BREWING

ELEVATOR BREWING COMPANY

THE PUB

How often do beer aficionados get to enjoy a handcrafted pint in a building recognized by the National Register of Historic Places? That distinction is but one of the many defining characteristics that distinguish the Elevator Brewery & Draught Haus in Columbus, OH.

Located at 161 N. High Street, the historic Columbia Building was erected in 1897 to house the Bott Brothers Cigars & Billiards. The Bott Brothers sold back-bars and billiards tables, and the business eventually evolved into a distillery and gentleman's saloon.

Echoes of the past abound today, to poignant effect. The Bott Brothers name remains etched above the front entry, tucked between the rounded display windows that once showed off the goods sold within. The original hand-carved Philippine mahogany bar, designed to serve the whiskey once distilled upstairs, glows warmly beneath the decorative ceiling, bathed in blue light. The mosaic tile floor and stained glass windows date back to the 1800s, as do the classic dartboards and antique billiards tables *(and yes, patrons are encouraged to play a game or two).* The exquisite back-bar won the blue ribbon for craftsmanship at the 1893 World Columbian Exposition in Chicago.

As for the four-star-rated menu and award-winning beer selection? They certainly complement the décor.

THE OWNER

Not many folks decide to open a brewpub at age 60. But Dick Stevens is no ordinary brewpub owner.

"And don't call it a crisis," he cautions with a wink, still barreling full steam ahead at age 74. "I still don't know what I want to do with my life."

Stevens, a larger-than-life character who refers to himself as the "Elevator Operator," established the Elevator Brewing Company in 1999 with his son, Ryan. This father-son beer-drinking team initially worked out of the small town of Marysville, OH, supplying eight custom brews to an attached restaurant. The brewery name was derived from the grain elevator building that housed the operation.

Constant struggles in Marysville inspired Stevens to establish his own brewpub in Columbus in 2000.

"I opened the restaurant to showcase our beer," he said. "It's as simple as that."

ATMOSPHERE
Stevens knew that his eatery needed to be much more than a standard brewpub. A visit to a brewers' convention hammered home a critical message: A brewpub can't build a reputation on pub food alone.

After securing the brewpub location, Stevens began to craft his dining vision: Art and ale. Spectacular paintings adorn the walls, immersed in color as the setting sun filters through the stained glass windows. It's a nod to the city's past; the art district to the north, the brewery district to the south, both united beneath a single downtown roof.

General Manager Will Triplett has been with the Elevator Brewery & Draught Haus for 11 of its 13 years in operation. He said the astonished reaction of first-time visitors never gets old.

"Most people are pretty blown away from the moment they walk in," Triplett said. "It's a

deceiving building; it seems a lot smaller from the exterior. It's a rare place, and most people have never been to a brewpub quite like it."

Perhaps the overall atmosphere is best represented by the company slogan: Elevate Your Taste.

"It's one of the most beautiful bars in the Midwest, and it's one of the most memorable dining experiences you'll ever have," Stevens said.

BEER & SPIRITS

Chris Yoha designs the innovative cocktail menu, which changes frequently. A popular favorite is the Grandview Highball, comprised of Watershed Distillery Gin, Domaine De Cantone, St. Germain and grapefruit juice.

"We do sell a ton of 'Barrel Bombs,' with our house-made root beer and Jagermeister," Triplett said.

One could argue that the main attraction at the restaurant is the handcrafted beer, a selection so extensive that it warrants its own menu. In addition to 12 beers served year-round, Elevator also pours seasonal favorites such as Horny Goat, a barrel-aged porter. And to further cement Elevator's status as a wildly creative enterprise, beer enthusiasts are challenged each year to earn their Masters of Beer Appreciation (*MBA*) and Professor of Hearty Drinking (*PHD*) degrees. Every month, Brewmaster Vic Schiltz and Assistant Brewer Mark Beery each release an extremely limited batch of a new, draft-only recipe. Featured beers this year include a Citrus Agave IPA and a Smoked Maple Nut Porter.

"We like to push the envelope a bit," Stevens explained. "I have two phenomenal brewers; why not turn them loose?"

CUISINE

In a twist of impeccable timing, a fine dining establishment called Liberty's went out of business just as Elevator was about to open. Stevens hired the entire kitchen staff from Liberty's to work at Elevator. One of the original kitchen staff members was Nathaniel Crockett, who quickly ascended from sous chef

to executive chef. Triplett credited Crockett's ingenuity as the inspiration behind Elevator's exceptional menu.

"We try to infuse beer in our cuisine as much as possible," Triplett explained. "There weren't a lot of beer-infused recipes out there when we started the restaurant." Crockett, a classically French-trained chef, adapted a number of recipes from wine to beer through a process of meticulous experimentation.

The results of Crockett's efforts flavor the entire menu. As an appetizer, Ryan's Corn Brats feature a pilsner-corn batter; the house chili is made with Bleeding Buckeye Red Ale; a Procrastinator Doppelbock demi-glace accompanies the Beef Tenderloin Medallions; and for dessert, Dirty Dick's Nut Brown Ale chocolate sauce is drizzled liberally atop brownies and cakes.

But the unequivocal gem of the menu is the Rock Filet, a cut-to-order tenderloin filet or Ahi tuna steak that diners cook themselves on a Tulikivi firestone. This distinctive flair emerged from a trip that Ryan took to Germany shortly before the restaurant opened.

After checking in on the German-engineered pilot brewhouse that had been commissioned for Elevator, Ryan enjoyed a memorable meal in Frankfurt where a steak was served on a searing stone – "but the Germans wouldn't tell him anything" about the method, Stevens said.

Undeterred, Ryan recreated the stone concept from memory. The Stevens also emailed the Geology Department at The Ohio State University to ask if anyone there was familiar with the cooking process; as it turned out, a well-traveled professor knew of a Finnish style of cooking meat on a soapstone. From there, it was just a matter of trial and error. The final touch: Stevens found a local artist to fashion a brand to sear the Elevator logo on each steak. And a signature dish was born.

ELEVATOR
BREWING COMPANY

Fitger's Brewhouse, Brewery & Grille

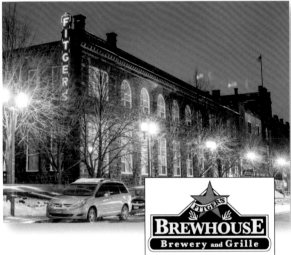

The Pub

Fitger's Brewhouse opened in 1995 on the shores of Lake Superior not long after owners Tim Nelson and Rod Raymond went on a ski trip and fell in love with the western U.S. brewing scene. By combining a relaxed Minnesota twist on the ski mountain brewpub with an uncompromising dedication to quality, Nelson and Raymond quickly established Fitger's Brewhouse as a cherished destination among Duluthians and Lake Superior North Shore tourists for hand-crafted beer, hearty pub fare with a healthy twist, and live music from local and touring artists.

Fitger's Brewhouse has won numerous national awards for its beer and become one of the largest brewpubs in the Midwest as measured by beer volume. The pub continues to push further to bring more localism and quality to its offerings, recently purchasing its own farm and cattle, which are grass fed and finished on spent grain from the brewery.

Owner

The building now known as the Fitger's Brewery Complex, which includes the Brewhouse Grille, Brewhouse Brewery and the Red Star Lounge, started its rich history in 1881 as part of Duluth's first and longest-operating brewery.

In 1857, Sidney Luce built Duluth's first brewery a block and a half from where the Fitger's Complex now stands on Superior Street. He chose this location partially because it allowed access to a small, clear run of water that eventually became known as Brewery Creek. By 1870 Luce had sold the operation to Nicholas Decker, who built a thriving business by featuring northeastern Minnesota's natural beauty in advertisements. Michael Fink, who owned the growing business by 1881, built a new and bigger brewery on the current Fitger's site. Fink's Lake Superior Brewing Company took on a young German brewmaster named August Fitger, who had recently graduated from one of his homeland's leading brewing schools. Within a year of being hired, Fitger owned half the company. In 1884 Percy Anneke, a traveling auditor for the Schlitz Brewing Company became Fitger's partner by buying half the Duluth operation which was then renamed the A. Fitger and Co. Lake Superior Brewery.

Over the next 40 years the brewery expanded to include 10 different buildings until Prohibition *(1920-1933)* drastically slowed the company's growth. Many U.S. breweries went under, but Fitger's stayed alive by producing soda pop and candy bars. During the Roaring Twenties candy lovers in Duluth and beyond enjoyed the Fitger's Flapper, the Fitger's Spark Plug, the 5-cent Fitger's Nut Goodie, the King Bee Nougat, and the Fitger's Skookum, "A bully good bar." The company's bottling house cranked out case after case of Lovit pop, a big favorite on summer Sunday picnics on Duluth's Park Point. After Prohibition Fitger's went back to brewing beer, and business boomed, growing to 100,000

barrels annually by 1940. In 1944 the brewery was bought by Duluth's Beerhalter family, who ran it until 1969. Fitger's Brewery closed its doors on September 30th, 1972. By 1995, when Tim Nelson and Rod Raymond opened Fitger's Brewhouse, the Fitger's Complex had been operating since the mid 1980s as a collection of shops and other businesses.

History and a sense of place is important to the Brewhouse. The group won a Minnesota Preservation Alliance award for restoration work at Tycoons Alehouse and the Rathskeller, which are located in the City Hall of Duluth's early years. In 1889, when the structure was first

built, Duluth had more millionaires per capita than anywhere else in the country. The group is currently working on the Endion Station Public House, located in an 1889 railroad depot, one of just two historic depots left in the city.

ATMOSPHERE

After being renovated to include a luxury hotel, retail spaces, and a brewing museum, the original Fitger's Brewery Complex was reopened in September 1984. The Brewhouse fits perfectly into the Complex's rustic-but-refined vibe that prominently features bluestone walls and giant support timbers. On any given evening, the Brewhouse might be filled with a lively mix of Carhartt-and-fleece-clad environmental education majors from the local University of Minnesota branch, well-heeled professionals, blue-collar workers, artists and musicians, and just about anyone in between. The later it gets, the more the crowd tends toward young adults who appreciate the Brewhouse's excellent beer and live music. Charlie Parr considers the Brewhouse his second home, and Trampled By Turtles played there before they hit it big. Lighting and music volume are always comfortable. Servers know their beers and their food, and are as warm and charming as they are professional. The general feeling is one of being in a super-cozy coffee shop that's been around for long enough to develop something like a soul.

BEER AND SPIRITS

Lead by Master Brewer Dave Hoops, the Brewhouse Brewery produces more than 80 styles and 3,000 barrels of fresh handcrafted beer every year. The company's various properties feature rotating combinations of 15 to 20 unique tap brews, between them, also available to go by the growler.

The Brewery's wide array of hand-crafted ales and lagers includes numerous award-winning brews: Starfire North Shore Pale Ale, El Niño IPA, Apricot Wheat, Witch Tree E.S.B., Big Boat Oatmeal Stout, Old World style cask conditioned ales *(including the Woodford Reserve Barrel-aged Edmund Imperial Stout and 1100 Wheat Wine)*, Farmhouse Saison, Fitger's Framboise, Wildfire Lager *(which is brewed with jalapenos and hatch chiles)*, and seasonal favorites such as the Celebration Cherry Batch *(made with local cherries)*. All the establishments feature full bars including quality wine selections.

CUISINE

Fitger's Brewhouse Grille serves a fresh menu of innovative comfort food and classic American grilled burgers and sandwiches, with strong health-conscious and vegetarian options that perfectly pair with the Brewery's beers and sodas. Executive Chef Dylan Westerlund prepares savory marinades, batters, and chutneys in-house to complement the locally raised beef, elk,

and fish served every day.

Starters include artichoke dip, authentic house-made hummus, blue chips with guacamole and salsa, and ultimate nachos made with a special vegetarian black bean chili. Creative salads are adorned with char-grilled chicken, portabella mushrooms, or smoked trout from Duluth's Northern Waters Smokehaus. Vegetarian entrées include black bean quesadillas and burritos, hummus wraps, and a satisfying burger made from a unique blend of traditionally harvested Minnesota wild rice.

Perhaps the most popular accompaniment to the Brewhouse's beers are its burgers, which come in part from Scottish Highland cattle from its own farm in Silver Bay, an hour northeast of Duluth along Lake Superior's North Shore. Char-grilled burgers of Wolf Creek elk, handmade salmon patties, Lake Superior lake trout, and savory local walleye are also served. Brewhouse burgers are served with fresh cheese, vegetables and creative chutneys and sauces made in house, along with heaping baskets of beer-battered traditional or sweet potato fries and onion rings.

Flat Branch Pub & Brewing

The Pub

Flat Branch Pub & Brewing is located at the heart of the historic district in downtown Columbia, Missouri. Flat Branch features craft beers made on-premise, a collection of single malt scotches and small-batch bourbons, and fresh and innovative comfort food in an old Studebaker car dealership. The building is complemented by a European-style beer garden, a sunny place of poetry in motion where patrons of all ages eat, drink and socialize amongst the trees and flowers of Columbia's favorite alfresco dining spot. Flat Branch, the city's first brewery since 1841, is popular for the wide range of award-winning ales and lagers it produces, as well as its great food, attentive service and casual everyone-is-family vibe.

Owner

Flat Branch Pub & Brewing was founded in 1994 by Tom Smith, who serves as president of the pub and chief "inventory reduction specialist". A serial entrepreneur, Smith also founded Datastorm Technogolies, a successful software company that was sold in 1996, and Sirius Hospitality, which operates multiple HuHot Mongolian Grill franchises. Friends say Tom has an adventurous and charismatic spirit; his next big life challenge isn't jumping "out of" or "off of" anything, but rather flying "into" space with Richard Branson's Virgin Galactic.

Smith's home base, Columbia, had been without a brewery since the mid-nineteenth century. By the early 1990s he recognized the growing demand for craft beers and the open market for a brewery in his hometown. At that time Smith was a craft beer enthusiast already home brewing and enjoying the local beers of different regions during his travels. Smith believed Columbians would embrace their own local brewery and pub house, and he was right. Flat Branch Pub & Brewing gave residents a craft beer brand to call their own, along with a family-friendly public house and beer garden for enjoying it, a place many now call their second home. Flat Branch has grown into an institution over the last two decades, and continues to serve as a central destination location for Mid-Missourians and out-of-towners, alike.

Tom and his guests rely on Flat Branch General Manager Lance Wood, Master Brewer Larry Goodwin, and a finely tuned management team and staff to keep the brewery and restaurant running smoothly, seven days a week.

ATMOSPHERE

This favorite Columbia watering hole is appropriately named for the nearby Flat Branch Creek, the main water source for early settlers to the area. Flat Branch occupies an old Studebaker car dealership in a 1927 brick warehouse, with vintage barrel-trussed roof and a spacious outdoor beer garden. The upscale industrial setting gives pub-goers a unique yet authentic tavern experience at one of Columbia's largest and most popular bars, while welcoming families and patrons of all ages with quality food, homemade sodas and stellar service. While the award-winning beers, crafted right on site, may draw the customers in, some believe it's the warm and friendly atmosphere, superior and heartily proportioned food, and fun that keeps them coming back.

Flat Branch has received more than its share of awards and recognition. It was named Best Brewery in Missouri three times by Rural Missouri Magazine; won Best Overall Restaurant the last four years running by the readers of Inside Columbia Magazine; received over 20 gold or silver awards by the same magazine in the five years of the poll's existence; called one of America's Best College Bars by Men's Health Magazine; and named one of the Best Bars in American by Esquire Magazine. And after a decade and a half's absence at the Great American Beer Festival, Flat Branch has taken home three silver medals in just two recent appearances at the world's most prestigious craft brewing festival.

BEER AND SPIRITS

The impressive Flat Branch brewing team has concocted more than 80 original craft beers in its time, producing 35-40 different varieties of beer each year, each with its own unique taste and following. The Honey Wheat is the most popular and easy to drink ale, made using American wheat ale and 30 pounds of honey to create a light and slightly sweet finish. The Oil Change Oatmeal Stout is as black as the used motor oil it is named for, and boasts dense roasted chocolate flavors. Golden naked oats give this stout its velvety smoothness, while nitrogen carbonation gives it a thick creamy head. The Oil Change Stout is among guests' favorite pours, and is also used in a variety of recipes, including the signature house dessert Stout Brownie Sundae. Flat Branch also features seasonal ales, fruit and pepper-infused brews, and rare beers, including an Imperial IPA featuring Nelson Sauvin and Galaxy hops, which came in at 11% ABV *(alcohol by volume)*, and the

GABF Silver Medal winning Baltic Rye Porter, a low bitterness, roasted malty porter made with significant portions of rye in the malt mix.

Flat Branch beers are finely crafted and lovingly tended. As Master Brewer Larry Goodwin says, "Flat Branch beers are made by Columbians, for Columbians". A minimum of 10 pub-brewed beers are featured on tap each day, often as many as 13, an unusually large selection for brewpubs. 18 ounces is the standard pour, but guests with lighter thirsts can opt for 10 ounces, or a sampler pack of 5 ounce glasses. Beer enthusiasts who fall in love with brews like the Katy Trail Pale Ale, Green Chili Beer, or other favorites can bring home a one-half gallon growler, five gallon pony keg or fifteen gallon half-barrel.

The bar at Flat Branch also features a broad selection of finely aged single-malt Scotch and small-batch Bourbon. Spirits drinkers can choose from over 40 mild to full-bodied whiskeys, including 10-year-old Lowlands, 15-year-old Highlands, a variety of Speysides, and the popular Glenfiddich Ancient Reserve. Scotch connoisseurs enjoy a taste of the Orkney Islands; sample the Isle of Mull; travel to a distillery established in 1786; and savor the Springbank, a classic Campbelltown whiskey made by the oldest family-owned distillery in Scotland. Featured Bourbons include the high 125 proof Booker's *(Jim Beam's grandson's personal recipe)*, the white oak barrel-aged Knob Creek, the unique Basil Hayden's, and Blanton's, one of the best single barrel bourbons produced.

CUISINE

Flat Branch offers patrons a choice of innovative comfort food and pub favorites with a fresh twist, using locally-sourced vegetables, and quality eggs and meats farm-raised in Mid-Missouri. Whenever possible, Flat Branch chooses cruelty free meats raised without antibiotics or growth hormones.

The pub has a from-scratch kitchen featuring an in-house bakery which delivers fresh breads and desserts straight from the oven. Patrons enjoy the legendary Flat Branch beer bread, homemade Kaiser-rolls, artisan buns, and the hearty barley bread boules served with their Chokes & Cheese, the rich and creamy artichoke cheese dip that regulars claim is addictive.

The pub features upscale versions of standard bar favorites like Buffalo chicken wings, piled high nachos, and sourdough brick-oven fired pizzas right alongside an elegant tomato and mushroom bisque. Hungry guests can feast on savory burgers and hot sandwiches with charbroiled chicken, house-smoked pulled pork and prime rib, and Missouri Legacy steak, while those with lighter appetites enjoy a selection of inventive salads made with seasonal greens and vegetables. Vegetarians crave the pub-made veggie burger with pesto and portabello mushroom with Boursin cheese sandwich.

With seasonal menu changes that rotate hearty winter favorites like Bangers and Mash and Shepherd's Pie with summer fare such as homemade bratwurst, Flat Branch entrees include hand-breaded catfish & chips, brown sugar cured pork chops, fall-off-the-bone baby back ribs, and a tasty meatloaf made with their own Oil Change Oatmeal Stout. Seafood lovers can enjoy grilled salmon, Ahi tuna, and fresh New England crab cakes, while dieters may prefer a no-gluten, no-dairy, low-carb Paleo Platter with choice of protein.

For the grand finale, Flat Branch bakers create spectacular meal-enders like the signature Stout Brownie Sundae and Crème Brule Bread Pudding. Inventive floats and sundaes are featured as well, made with Mizzou's own Arbuckles Ice Cream, and Flat Branch sodas and stouts.

As the wide variety of people lined up out the door on weekends attests, Flat Branch truly has something for everyone to enjoy.

FRANKENMUTH BREWERY

THE PUB

The Frankenmuth Brewery was founded in 1862, and is one of the oldest breweries in the country, celebrating 151 years of Michigan's original craft beer. Re-opened under new ownership on July 1, 2009, this historic brewery now includes two American-style indoor restaurants with three patios overlooking the scenic Cass River. The 28,000 square foot German-styled microbrewery serves high-value classic meals, handcrafted Old World crafted beers and Root Bier and select wines to the residents and guests of Michigan's Little Bavaria. Today, Frankenmuth Brewery's award-winning lagers and ales are sold by distributors throughout Michigan and five other surrounding states.

HISTORY

Frankenmuth's first settlers brought the tradition of authentic German brewing to mid-Michigan in 1845. John Matthias Fallier founded the city's first brewery in 1857. Cousins William Knaust and Martin Heubisch opened the Cass River Brewery just north of the Fallier brewery in 1862, in the exact spot where the Frankenmuth Brewery continues to stand today. The Cass River Brewery was purchased by Johann Geyer in 1874 and renamed Geyer's Brothers Brewing Co. For the next 112 years, the facility operated under many names and owners, eventually being renamed the Frankenmuth Brewing Company. Ferdinand Schumacher from Duseldorf, Germany purchased the brewery one year before a fire destroyed most of the structure in 1987. Randall E. Heine rebuilt the brewery and resumed its operation in 1990. The historic microbrewery was at peak production by 1996, distributing more than 30,000 barrels of locally produced microbrews across 25 states when an F3 tornado struck the facility, destroying the operation once again. Another six years would pass before the brewery was reopened, this time with the addition of a three-level brew pub. Due to economic reasons, the doors to Frankenmuth Brewery were closed again in 2006.

Entrepreneur Anmar K. Sarafa, his brother Haithem and a couple of partners purchased the historic operation and re-opened the doors to Frankenmuth's beloved brewery on July 1, 2009. Committed to the economic health of his community, the Sarafa's hired a large team of managers and employees from the area, negotiated with a state-wide distributorship

network, and revitalized "the jewel of Frankenmuth", restoring the rich history, traditions and pride of this Michigan landmark for residents and visitors alike, to enjoy once again.

ATMOSPHERE

The Frankenmuth Brewery stands four stories tall in its original spot on the Cass River in downtown Frankenmuth, dating back to 1862. Located in the thriving pedestrian-friendly community of Little Bavaria, this historic waterfront brewery and restaurant is an exciting destination for food lovers and beer aficionados alike. The 28,000 square foot red-brick building features the microbrewery operation and two restaurants with indoor seating for 432 guests, complete with outdoor patios on three levels and seating for another 250 guests. A plethora of private dining rooms are available for banquets, business meetings and other special events, along with a gift shop full of fun memorabilia and craft beers for home enjoyment. Patrons of the brewhouse include a large number of locals who cherish the authenticity of their own craft brand, along with the many visiting tourists of the historic German town, passengers of the Bavarian Belle Riverboat, and nearby shoppers from the renowned River Place Shopping Village. Guests of all ages are graciously welcomed to learn all about authentic Old World brewing and bottling with free daily tours of the brewery featured, and even opportunities to become a brewmaster for the day.

Beer and Spirits

Brewmaster Jeff Coon produces over 2,000 barrels of six year-round crafted ales and lagers for patrons to enjoy at their restaurants and bars, or at home in to-go growlers. This authentic and traditional Old World German-styled microbrewery crafts its lagers and ales according to the German Beer Purity Laws, producing award-winning brews cherished and now sold by distributors throughout the state of Michigan. The Frankenmuth Pilsener is their flagship beer, made in the old German tradition. The American Blonde Ale is a cross over ale made with American malts and fermented at a lower temperature to create a clean mellow finish. Frankenmuth's Hefeweizen is a wheat based, sweet and refreshing, traditional German summer ale with naturally occurring hints of clove and banana. Frankenmuth's Red Sky is a full-flavored Irish-style red ale made with roasted barley, subtle caramel notes and a malt finish, and the perfect accompaniment to hearty cuisine. The Batch 69 American-Style India Pale Ale is a medium light-bodied India Pale Ale with an intense hop aroma and flavor, with hints of citrus, flowers and pine. It pairs well with spicy food and sweet desserts. The Munich Style Dunkel Lager is named for the city it calls home. This classic German lager has a distinguished dark appearance and a notably smooth sweet balanced flavor, a favorite pairing with hearty pork dishes and rich chocolate desserts. Frankenmuth seasonal brews are also introduced throughout the year and include: Oktoberfest, Harvest Ale, Winter Bock and Baltic Porter. Other specialty beers, sold in 1 liter bottles, include Imperial Stout, J.B. McGinnis Dry Irish Stout and a 150 Anniversary Dark Lager.

The Brewery also produces Frankie's Root Bier, brewed in-house with the same patience and craftsmanship as the award-winning beers. The Root Bier is made in small batches, sweetened with Michigan beet sugar and pure vanilla to create a splash of flavors along with its unmistakable bite. Like Frankenmuth's six year-round brews, Frankie's Root Bier is available in the bottle by six-pack or the case.

Cuisine

The Frankenmuth Brewery features two restaurants with plenty of indoor and outdoor seating to feed the town, and a classic pub food menu to please every diner's palate. Frankemuth handcrafted beers are conveniently paired with all of the offerings and incorporated into a large variety of the dishes served. A warm Bavarian pretzel bread highlights the award-winning Hefeweizen, while the Brewers' Bread is made from brewery grains and three cheeses. Traditional pub favorites of hearty nachos, beer-battered onion rings, and savory chicken wings are served along with creative buffalo chicken rolls and portabella fries made with the Dunkel craft lager.

Fresh soups and salads are featured daily and include a Michigan Navy Bean soup and a traditional French Onion made with Dunkel. Hand-tossed made to order pizzas, and burgers made of Choice Angus Beef are among the popular selections. Healthier alternatives include a gluten-free wheat pizza crust, and burger patties of turkey or low-fat Certified Piedmontese Beef. A variety of fresh sandwiches and wraps are featured, including a Michigan Cherry and Chicken Wrap, and a traditional grilled German bratwurst served with spicy mustard and sauerkraut in a fresh hoagie roll.

Frankenmuth entrees run the gamut in hearty comfort food, incorporating fresh and local ingredients into many of the dishes. The Mountain-High Meatloaf Sandwich, slow smoked Baby Back Ribs, and Fish and Chips made with Dunkel-battered Cod are brewhouse mainstays. Sirloin Filets, traditional and chipotle-seasoned, Cajun Salmon and panko-crusted Parmesan Chicken are served with white cheddar potatoes and seasonal vegetables. Diners

also enjoy a wide range of pastas, including a Shrimp Linguine, Four Cheese Ravioli and house Macaroni and Cheese.

Frankenmuth desserts include decadent pies made with creamy peanut butter and chocolate, lemon berry mascarpone, or apples and caramel. Generous slices of NY Style Raspberry or Red Velvet Cheesecake, and German Chocolate Cake satisfy any sweet tooth. The signature Dog Bowl Dessert features hand-tossed pizza dough, fried and dusted in cinnamon and sugar, served with ice cream, whipped cream and a special house-made chocolate Frankie. Home-made Root Bier floats and fried sweet dough Oreos round out the list of perfect meal-enders.

If you are ever in Frankenmuth, this is one place you won't want to miss.

Hoppy Brewing Company

The Pub

Hoppy has been a landmark in East Sacramento since moving into what was formerly an old feed store on June 1, 1999. It features vaulted ceilings, a stunning view of the brewery, stained wood, plants in a well-lit environment, with friendly staff, and TV's featuring sports, news & weather most of the day. The bar is 40 feet long with 17 seats that are usually filled with regulars bantering about various current events. Hoppy features nine beers on tap that are made on-premise, along with locally sourced wine and top-shelf liquor for customers to enjoy while winding down from a day of hard work, or even to celebrate some special occasion. It is located near Sacramento State University, Caltrans Headquarters, and SMUD Headquarters and University California at Davis Medical Center.

Owners

Troy Paski graduated from the University of Georgia with a BS in Physics in 1984 and moved to California to work at Lockheed operating satellites for the government. Having gained experience in satellite operations, and software debugging/development, he started a company that was originally conceived with the intentof providing engineering services to the defense industry. However, as an avid home brewer since receiving a brewing kit for Christmas in 1991, and having a passion for truly great beer, he soon realized a much more lucrative growth opportunity emerging in the craft-brewing industry.

On a chilly autumn evening in 1993, while sampling a blueberry it was officially decided to focus his energy on commercially marketing his company's new flagship product, which up until then had been T.ROY's home-brew specialty. It took him six months to find the right investors and suppliers before he was able to debut his flagship product at the California Small Brewers Festival in Mountain View, California in 1994.

In an attempt to carve out a niche in the growing microbrewery market, he decided to distinguish the company from the competition by providing the consumer with an easily identifiable package that was unlike anything ever seen, along with a traditional style of beer that had not been readily available to consumers for quite some time. He believed this type of

beer tended to attract those consumers who were currently drinking hand-crafted pale ales, and who were looking for a fuller-bodied "more mouth feel" type of beer to drink.

ATMOSPHERE

Hoppy Brewing Company is located in what used to be the original farmers feed and supply store for East Sacramento. The large industrial building houses the microbrewery, restaurant and bar, providing locals with an intimate and family friendly restaurant dining experience. Hoppy caters to its locals, the bread and butter of its success, and ground-zero launching point for the large following of Hoppy's craft beers

nationwide. Hoppy hosts many community activities, fundraisers, special events and entertainment each week, and is a favorite eatery for it's upscale, yet value oriented, food and award-winning beers served in a friendly casual atmosphere.

BEER AND SPIRITS

Hoppy produces 450 gallons of hand-crafted beer per batch on premise at the microbrewery, served fresh in the restaurant each day. The locals enjoy their own craft beers from the tap in 3 ounce samplers, a 16 ounce pint glass, or a 20 ounce mug if you are lucky enough to be a member, while beer enthusiasts in 17 states around the country savor their Hoppy ales largely by the 22 ounce bomber bottle.

The craft beers of Hoppy are divided into three product lines: Lights, Mediums, and Darks; along with two Brewers Specials each month. The Lights include Golden Nugget Cream Ale, Liquid Sunshin Blonde Ale, and Heff-a's weizen. The Golden Nugget is their lightest ale, fermented with ale yeast at lager temperatures to produce a smooth brew, balanced with Munich Malts and Vanguard Hops. Liquid Sunshine Blonde Ale features a generous dose of Crystal Hops which lend their grapefruit-like flavor and aroma. It is a very refreshing brewer's favorite that is also available in draft and bottles off-premise. Heff-a – Weizen is a 50/50 blend of Wheat and Barley Malts fermented with an authentic Bavarian Weizen yeast for traditional banana and clove-like dryness. Hopped with just enough German-style hops to balance the malt and served unfiltered.

The Mediums include Hoppy Face Amber Ale and Burnt Sienna Ale. The Hoppy Face Amber Ale is a big amber ale, much like the first IPA from the dawn of the Industrial Revolution. A blend of Caramel Malts give this beer a rich yet highly drinkable body, and heavy-handed additions of Nugget, Cascade, and Liberty Hops protect this beer for the long cruise to India. Burnt Sienna Ale is brewed with Pale, Caramel and Smoked Malts with a hint of roasted barley. It is hopped and re-hopped and hopped again with Columbus, Glacier, and Willamette Hops.

The Darks include Stony Face Red Ale and Total Eclipse Black Ale. The Stony Face Red Ale – is Hoppy's gift to those who like their beers malty. Dark Caramel and Chocolate Malts lend their deep crimson silkiness, and judicious additions of Nugget and Cascade Hops give just enough bitterness for balance. Ask your server's favorite beer and it's probably this one. Total Eclipse Black Ale is robust, and features Chocolate and Black Malts for a dark-roasted coffee-like flavor. It is hopped with a-shade-more-than-typical additions of Nugget and Columbus Hops for an assertive yet still pleasant bitterness. Both are available in draft and bottles off-premise as well. Hoppy features locally sourced wines from nearby Napa and Amador counties, and an elite "top-shelf" selection of distilled spirits for those

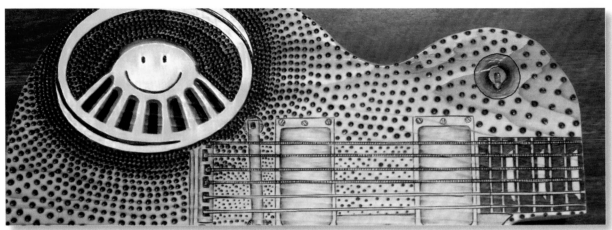

who do not appreciate a quality craft beer as an alternative to help provide a bit of relaxation.

CUISINE

Hoppy provides diners with a value oriented menu for brunch, lunch, and dinner, featuring classic American grilled Bison steaks, seafood, portabellas, chicken, ribs and burgers. Starters include traditional finger-food like Hoppy's famous fresh-cut Kettle Chips or Fries and house-made dipping sauces, Nachos, Buffalo Chicken Wings and Fried Calamari, plus a seared Sesame Ahi Tuna, Bison Hot Dogs, and five different sliders.

The menu features a wide assortment of fresh salads and greens topped with Chicken, Prawns, or Ahi, Jerk Marinated Pork Loins, Bison Rib-Eye steak, two daily house-made soups served by the cup or bowl, 12 inch whole-grain pizza and various pastas.

Favorites include the build your own Burger and an ale-battered Codfish with fresh chips.

Inventive tortilla wraps with seared Ahi, or even spicy BBQ Baby Back Ribs marinated in their own Stony Face Red Ale, not to mention a Salmon Pesto pasta.

A special Brunch menu is featured on weekends and holidays, introducing hot favorites of Hoppy Breakfast, with your choice of meat, style of eggs, starch, & toast, pancakes, omelets, grits, eggs, and hash browns, paired with a Mimosa, or top-shelf Bloody Mary.

Hoppy's features a dessert menu of house-made items such as: Seasonal Fruit Crisp, Oreo Brownie Sunday, Chocolate Mousse, Lemon Pie, Bread Pudding, Crème Brulee or even a scoop of Vanilla Bean Ice Cream.

HORSE & HOUND GASTROPUB

THE PUB

The chef owned and operated Horse & Hound Gastropub is located in pedestrian-friendly midtown Charlottesville, catering to local residents, UVA college students and the historical city's many visiting tourists. Horse & Hound serves fresh, upscale, gourmet pub fare; each dish carefully paired with craft beers from around the world, and boutique wines from Virginia's wineries. Celebrating scent hounds and field hunters, the traditional 16th-century hunt-styled gastropub provides a relaxed setting where patrons taste their way through four courses of the latest culinary trends, enjoy a pint on the patio with their dog, or discover the city's latest musical group with friends.

OWNERS

The talent behind the scenes of the Horse & Hound Gastropub is husband and wife founders, owners and partners, Executive Chef Luther Fedora, and Pastry Chef Brooke Fedora. The two first met at the Culinary Institute of America in Hyde Park, where they both attended in the 90's. After college, Luther spent the next several years abroad, formally training in France, discovering his passion for craft beers, and fine-tuning his wine knowledge in England. Luther worked for world-class establishments, including the Savoy Hotel, and the Michelin-starred Drones of London, owned by British celebrity, Chef Marco Pierre White. Brooke moved to New York after college, where she spent the next several years honing her skills as a pastry chef, creating confections at Michael's in Manhattan and working at The River Café in Brooklyn. Ready for a change of pace from the big city life, the couple moved to Charlottesville in 2003, married, and opened their dream restaurant in June 2007. The Fedoras styled the Horse & Hound as a gastropub, the hottest new food trend from Great Britain. Their mission, to provide guests with a comfortable atmosphere for experiencing affordable, fresh, innovative food and artisan draughts of a fine-dining quality. Luther serves as Executive Chef and runs the back of the house, while Brooke works as the Pastry Chef, manages the front of the house, and runs the catering side of the business. The Fedoras share a home with their young son, Quinn, in Earlysville, where they maintain an organic garden, growing many of the vegetables they serve fresh.

ATMOSPHERE

Horse & Hound Gastropub is located on West Main Street in the downtown commercial district of Charlottesville called "Midtown". The University of Virginia, Downtown Mall, and many businesses, bars, restaurants, museums, music venues and retail shops occupy the thriving community hub. This area hosts 21,500 UVA college students, and countless vacationers to the city's many historic sites, and craft breweries and wineries. The British-influenced Horse & Hound Gastropub features distinctive libations, dinners and brunch at natural wooden tables and booths in the dining room and separate bar, adorned with traditional horse and hound hunting motif and artwork. A picturesque patio garden provides diners with comfortable outdoor seating under large umbrellas, with portable heaters added during the winter. The restaurant offers a wide range of special event services, including event planning, catering *(on or off-premise)*, barbecue dinners, and full-service weddings, including gorgeous one-of-a-kind cakes made by Brooke and her team. While the upscale décor, food and liquor reflect the Fedoras unmistakable passion for food and their commitment to quality, the Horse & Hound has the relaxed ambience and neighborhood appeal of an authentic community pub house.

BEER AND SPIRITS

Horse & Hound Gastropub features extensive beer and wine menus, pairing each of their culinary creations, including Chef Brooke's decadent desserts, with a unique selection of liquid assets. There are 28 bottled beer varieties, including a few of the classics, while 13 unique draught beers are served fresh from the tap in 9 and 16 ounce glasses, liters and pitchers, and include tasting flights of 4, 8, and 12 beers in 6 ounce pours. Current artisan draughts include: a wildflower honey and blood orange Slumbrew Happy Sol Hefewiezen; the surprisingly floral North Coast Pranqster Belgium Strong Golden Ale; and the double-pilsner Breckenridge Regal

Imperial. The authentic German Apostelbrau Dinkel Bock and the original Paulaner Salvatore Doppleback are popular, along with the Allagash Fluxus, a strong pale ale brewed with spiced green and pink peppercorns. The Ommegang Art of Darkness is a Belgium Strong dark ale, full of mystique in flavor and champagne-like carbonation, while the Wolaver's Alta Gracia Coffee Porter finishes with strong flavors from organic vanilla beans and coffee from the Dominican Republic.

During his travels through Europe, Luther discovered his love for artisan beers, along with the social traditions surrounding them. Horse

& Hound patrons enjoy endless pours of Kolsch from Cologne, Germany, served traditional in a special 12-glass circular tray called a Kranz. In keeping with the Kobesin, empty glasses are replaced intuitively by the staff, until a beer mat is placed over each glass to signal end of service.

The Horse & Hound wine menu headlines sparkling, white and red varieties produced locally by boutique vineyards in Virginia. Featured vineyards include Michael Shaps, Horton, Pollak, Veritas, Gabriele Rausse and King Family, along with The Williamsburg Winery and Gadino Cellars.

CUISINE

Meals at the Horse & Hound beautifully reflect Chef Fedoras' ethos, with extraordinary time and effort in creating everything from scratch, using fresh, organic and well-sourced ingredients. Diners enjoy an evolving offering of gourmet starters, salads, soups, entrees and desserts. Popular three and four course dinners paired with their beers provide guests with a new culinary journey, from week to week. The first course features imaginative plates of Dungeness Crab Salad, Fried Oysters, Smoked Beef Tartar and Mini Lamb Kabobs. Chef Luther's original entrees include Pan Seared Scallops, Stuffed Roasted Lamb Leg, Confit Chicken and Chorizo Stuffed Pork Lion. Chef Brooke's desserts are as beautiful as they are delicious, and include a Thousand Layer Cake, Salted Caramel Crème Brulee, Burnt Pineapple Mouse, Lemon Gelato wrapped in meringue

to create individual baked Alaska and Dark Chocolate cream with chocolate lace Cookies. Flights of artisan cheeses like Morbier, Smoked Gouda, and Double Gloucester with Chives are served with an apple chutney and ciabatta toast.

Jackie O's Pub and Brewery

The Pub

Jackie O's Pub and Brewery is the first and only Brewpub located in the downtown historic district of Athens, Ohio. Jackie O's serves as an important watering hole for Athenians, 20,000 Ohio University students and their guests. Producing over 60 handcrafted artisan ales each year; each pint is infused with American creativity, locally grown ingredients, and traditional brewing techniques. Jackie O's dedication to locally grown and produced goods is apparent in every aspect of its products by supporting over 20 farms, creameries and orchards in Ohio.

The Owners

Owners of a successful Athens bagel shop, Bagel Street Deli, Art Oestrike, Lenny Meyer and Megan Meyer decided it was time to pursue their dream of owning and managing a bar. A local brewpub, O'Hooley's, had fallen on hard times and was in need of new management. This was the opportunity Oestrike and the Meyers were looking for. Having frequented the brewpub for many years, Oestrike and the Meyers had formed a close relationship with the owner, Jim Prouty, and expressed their interest in acquiring the business. Prouty was overjoyed to pass the business on to the Athenian entrepreneurs, and on December 12, 2005, the deli owners became proud new brewpub owners. In 2009, Oestrike, the primary owner of the burgeoning Jackie O's empire, purchased the adjacent bar/restaurant and has enjoyed great success ever since.

The Atmosphere

Jackie O's is a popular hang out for Athenians, Ohio University students, faculty and tourists. Connected by a sprawling patio, the two sides of Jackie O's offer dining, beer tasting, and entertainment space for hundreds of patrons. It's beautifully inlayed tables and hand-made chairs make it a cozy destination for all that want to enjoy fine craft beers, locally and sustainably grown meals or live shows. The large "Public House" side is a favorite venue for local and national acts that entertain guests throughout the week and weekend while the more intimate "Brewpub" side offers a relaxed dining, beer tasting environment and, of course, the original brewery.

THE BEER

With 40 beers on tap, Jackie O's offers an ale for every pallet. House favorites include Firefly Amber Ale, Razz Wheat, Chomolungma Honey Nut Brown, Mystic Mama IPA and Hop Ryot Rye IPA. Brew Master Brad Clark's unorthodox brewing techniques and ingredients have captured the admiration of thousands of craft beer fans. Some of his unusual infusions include the use of pawpaw fruit, black walnuts, maple syrup, spice bush, lemon verbena, coffee, pumpkins, and much more. Clark has also dedicated a large portion of his craft to barrel aging and souring. Fan favorites include Bourbon Barrel Dark Apparition Russian Imperial Stout, Rum Barrel Brick Kiln Barley Wine and Cab Cherryman, a Cabernet Barrel-Aged Cherry Porter. These and other world-renowned brews have catapulted Jackie O's into the adored brewery it is today. Throughout 2012 and 2013, Sean White has begun and will continue to take over the reins at the original facility while Clark moves to a different role as "Head of Brewing Operations" for both facilities.

THE CUISINE

Focusing on organically grown and produced foods, Jackie O's partners with as many Athens County farms, orchards, and creameries as possible. This "locavore" devotion is so engrained

in the Jackie O's mission that in 2010 owner Art Oestrike purchased a 20 acre farm outside of downtown Athens to ensure the quality and freshness of all of Jackie O's menu items. The constantly evolving menu features classic pub food with a fresh, local twist. Items such as pizza dough infused with spent grain and beef from cattle that were raised on spent grain make this menu truly unique and delicious. The Jackie O's bakery produces all of the bread used in house, including gluten-free options. In addition to artisan pizzas and burgers, Jackie O's patrons rave about menu favorites such as O'Hooley's Fish and Chips and a savory local Laurel Valley Creamery Cheese Plate featuring crackers baked fresh to order with homemade tapenade and hummus on the side. One bite of anything on the Jackie O's menu provides evidence to the ongoing commitment to providing the freshest, organically grown local menu items prepared with the utmost care and attention.

The Production Facility

Opened in early 2013, the Jackie O's Production Facility and Taproom is home of the first craft beer canning operation in the state of Ohio. This offsite location located in downtown Athens, Ohio, allows Jackie O's to grow and distribute its magnificent craft brews to bars and grocery stores all over the state of Ohio and beyond.

Jackie O's
PUB & BREWERY
athens, OHIO

LaTrappe Café, Belgian Bistro & Trappist Lounge

The Pub

LaTrappe Café is a Belgian Bistro & Trappist Lounge located in San Francisco's Little Italy, also commonly known as North Beach. Adjacent to Chinatown, Fishermen's Wharf and Russian Hill, North Beach is the historic center of beatnik subculture, a classic nightlife destination, and one of ten "Great Neighborhoods in America", full of young urban professionals. The cozy brick-cellar setting of LaTrappe Café welcomes an eclectic mix of guests to experience the ambience of Belgium, and celebrate the world's most unique and flavorful beers handcrafted by Trappist monks, dating back over 1,000 years. LaTrappe Café features an evolving menu of 300 of the most celebrated artisan beers from Europe, rivaled only by its pairing with meticulous Belgian-styled gastropub fare.

Owners

LaTrappe Café was opened on December 4, 2007, in the old Buca Giovanni location at 800 Greenwich Street. Owner, Michael Azzalini's great grandfather, Joseph Foppiano, purchased the historic building in 1928, and used the cool basement to age his wine during The Prohibition Era. The two-story, red-brick structure has had a rich history over the past century, also housing a dance studio, dental office, and The Rolling Wheels *(hot rods)* Club run by Michael's uncle in the 1950s, before finally finding its niche as a neighborhood restaurant. After years of watching Italian restaurants come and go, Azzalini decided San Francisco's Little Italy was ready for something unique, something Belgian. Fondly modeled after his favorite brasseries and beer bars in Antwerp, Bruges, Brussels and Ghent, Azzalini transformed the North Beach storefront restaurant into one of the hottest new gastropubs on the west coast, with a distinct Belgian voice. With a genuine affinity for high-quality beer, "the great, non-aristocratic, democratic drink", La Trappe showcases over 400 bottled beers and another fifteen fresh from rotating taps, along with authentic Belgian gastronomic specialties, like rabbit stew, mussels in beer and twice-cooked Frites. Mike Azzalini attributes much of LaTrappe's popularity and success to neighborhood residents, a large and important part of their customer base; locals, who by all accounts, have spread the word about this hopping Belgian Bistro & Lounge, like wildfire.

ATMOSPHERE

LaTrappe Café is ideally located at the corners of Greenwich, Mason and Columbia, with a Walk Score of 89 out of 100. The Mason St. Cable Car runs in both directions, stopping directly in front of the restaurant for patrons not on foot. A warm storefront welcomes patrons into the upstairs dining room of the Belgian Bistro, with deep wooden floors, light walls trimmed in salmon accents and bright open windows. An assortment of 2 and 4-top, elegantly-dressed tables are featured, along with the spacious bar-top, providing every diner with optimal views of San Fran's busy pedestrian-friendly streets, and the exhibition kitchen. A beautiful winding staircase leads patrons downstairs into the cellar and now famous, Trappist Lounge. Bricked walls, arched ceilings and muted lighting create the intimate ambience of an authentic European brasserie, that's anything but silent.

BEER

French and Flemish abbeys began brewing artisan beers as a source of income, dating back to the first crusades in 1096. Belgium's Westmalle is the first Trappist brewery established 50 years after the Revolution, in 1836. The Trappist creed comes from the Rule of St. Benedict stating "for then are they monks in truth, if they live by the work of their hands". As a result of strict

adherence for the last 1,000 years plus, Trappist monks produce a wealth of high-quality goods to support their 170 monasteries in the world today, and are world renowned for their unique artisan beers. Trappist beers are deep flavorful beers that contain residual sugar and living yeast, and much like fine wine, actually improves with age.

Staying true to their inspirations, Mike Azzalini headlines 400 Belgian year-round bottled beers, feature another 30 seasonal crafts, and serve 15 fresh from revolving taps at their Trappist Lounge. Beer drinkers journey across the pond, tasting Blonde and Brune from the

Achel monastery; Red, White and Blue Labels from Chimay; dry-hopped amber from Orval; decadent darks from Rochefort; Green, Blonde, Blue and Yellow Caps from Westvleteren, and unmistakable Dubbel and Tripel from the world's oldest Trappist monastery, Westmalle. Each of the 300 beers featured is served in its artisan bottle or in authentic glassware created specifically to highlight its unique qualities. Elegant beer tastings and dinners are provided to educate and celebrate each new star.

CUISINE

The Belgian gastropub showcases the Pacific's fresh bounty with Belgian-styled dishes,

complimenting their extraordinary beers with an equally extraordinary cuisine. The classically-trained chef procures artisan ingredients local, from other sustainable and quality-committed businesses in San Francisco. The fresh seafood served is brought in fresh daily, from I Love Blue Sea at the Fisherman's Wharf. Organic poultry and meats are sourced from Biagio Artisan Meats, Fallon Hills Ranch, Marin Sun Farms and Avedano's Holly Park Market.

Popular sliders and twice-cooked Belgian Fries and Frites feature 10 inventive dipping sauces, from Belgian and Andalouse mayos to Chipotle ketchup. Starters of Kale & Smoked Sausage and Smoked Trout Tartine burst with flavor and technique, while fresh oysters and inventive mussel platters are always among the rave. A new soup is featured each day, along with creative salads dressed in spicy vinaigrettes, and topped with seared sashimi-grade tuna and fresh anchovies.

A new seafood entree is served daily, along with mussel mainstays, like the Moules a la Bier, mussels in dark ale sauce, or slow-cooked in a spicy tomato sauce, both served with house Belgian fries and dipping sauces. Traditional Belgian stews include the Seafood Waterzooi, made with manila clams, mussels and local fish fillet, and the Carbonnade a la Flamande, made from beef marinated in gueuze, and finished with dark ale. Roasted free-range chicken is served inside puff pastry in the Chicken Videe-Voulevant, while Flemish Chicken is sautéed in onions, carrots, celery, spices and a cherry ale sauce, served traditional on the bone with mashed potatoes. Meat lovers savor organic grass-fed beef and pork in Spaghetti Bolognese, gourmet hamburgers and Ribeye steaks.

Check the time of year for your visit, for their gourmet-class cuisine changes with every season.

Note: La Trappe Cafe, Belgian Bistro and Trappist Lounge has no affiliation with La Trappe Trappist Beer

MOAB BREWERY

THE PUB

Moab Brewery is home to the only microbrewery in Moab, Utah, and one of the town's most successful restaurants. This landmark brewery handcrafts ten signature ales and lagers served fresh from the tap. They also offer five styles in their high gravity Desert Select Ale series, and three signature beers available in 16 oz cans. Moab Brewery product is offered throughout the state of Utah, as well as Idaho, Nevada, Maryland, Delaware and Washington D.C. They will potentially be branching into California, Colorado, Arizona and Mississippi. In addition to its popular brews, Moab Brewery serves a large diverse menu of pub cuisine for lunch and dinner, seven days a week, along with its handcrafted root beer and house-made Italian gelatos. This bright and lively tavern is a cool oasis for Moab's large community of runners, cyclists, hikers, and bikers (*mountain*

and Harleys), catering to its large customer base of locals, as well as the many visiting tourists of the nearby Arches, Canyonlands National Parks and annual Moab Jeep Safari.

OWNERS

Moab Brewery was founded in 1996 by partners, John Borkoski and Dave Sabey (*Dave appreciates a good beer anywhere)*. Restaurateur John Borkoski opened his first brewery in McCall, Idaho in 1993. They both discovered the untapped market for craft beers in Utah's conservative state and saw the potential for a local watering hole in the budding community in Moab, Utah. Committed to produce only high quality food and libations, the two founded Moab's microbrewery, building a balanced family atmosphere to meet the needs of all residents. Borkoski and Sabey launched a third brewpub in Logan, Utah. Beehive Grill opened its doors in June 2009, serving the same successful recipe of beloved craft food and libations, while becoming Logan's only on-site Root Beer Brewery.

ATMOSPHERE

Originally settled as a Silver Boom Town, the dramatic landscape of Moab, Utah is celebrated today for its spectacular adventure recreation in one of the largest outdoor playgrounds for hikers, mountain bikers and river rafters in the southwest. The Moab Brewery is located on South Main in a spacious adobe-styled building, housing a large restaurant, a separate bar and retail store, along with the microbrewery

Jeff Van Horn, Head Brewer

53

operation. The sun-filled brewery is painted in soft sandstone and trimmed in all natural wood, creating a bright and airy oasis. The walls and ceilings are adorned with adventure gear from local outfitters, and include mountain bikes, kayaks, a hang glider and even a novelty Jeep. Murals depicting the wildlife and red rock scenery of the surrounding pristine wilderness welcome explorers to exceptional food and libations after a day on the trails. An enclosed patio with open windows *(weather permitting)* is perfect for enjoying cool desert evenings. A glass wall in the tavern provides patrons with an atrium view of the craft brewing operation and pride of Moab.

BEER AND SPIRITS

While the Moab Brewery has a full liquor license and sells assorted spirits and wines, the local-made brews are this brewpub's trademark. Moab Brewery handcrafts 17 signature year-round ales and lagers. They always have ten beers on tap, and brew an additional five for their Desert Select Ale series which are bottled onsite. They also offer 16 oz cans of Four percent in session brews which include Dead Horse Amber, Johnny's American IPA and Rocket Bike American Lager. Johnny's IPA and Rocket Bike are also served canned at full strength. All of the brewing takes place in a 7,000 square foot brewing and canning facility. The Brewery produces 10,000

barrels of beer each year, now sold by the keg, bottle and 16 ounce cans throughout Utah. Since the expansion of their brewery in 2011, they are rapidly branching into multiple states and their product can be found in hundreds of locations across the country.

Moab Brewery's signature brews range in flavor from the a classic Baja Especial Wheat Ale, to the Black Raven Stout, a hearty oatmeal stout with a creamy start and crisp finish. The popular Porcupine Pilsner is a flavorful German-styled lager, lightly hopped with a touch of wheat. Over the Top Hefeweizen is a refreshing American wheat served unfiltered with a lemon slice. One of the most popular pours is the Dead Horse Amber Ale, a mild English ale named after a scenic overlook in the Canyonlands. The Rocket Bike American Lager is a unique steamer-style lager, brewed with a special strain of lager yeast and techniques dating back to the 1800s. The vibrant citrus and bitterness of Johnny's American IPA are created by four bold American hops, while the Scorpion Pale Ale's six hops are mild in color, yet carry a sting. Derailleur Ale has a complex profile of six malts and four hearty hops, creating a smooth downhill ride. The unique line of bottle-conditioned Desert Select Ales includes a Black Imperial IPA, Tripel, Scotch IPA, Export Stout and Hopped Rye, each

tipping the scales at almost 9% alcohol content.

Like the ales, Root Beer and a variety of carbonated sodas flavored with black cherry, grape, orange cream and pink pomegranate lemonade are made on-premise. The nostalgic and renowned Beehive Root Beer is made with a spicy blend of root beer, sarsaparilla and cane sugar, and is the headliner at the Beehive Grill in Logan, and sold throughout Utah.

CUISINE

Moab Brewery features a large diverse food menu of pub cuisine, incorporating and pairing each dish with its award-winning craft beverages. Patrons enjoy a plethora of creative finger foods, smoked items, fresh salads and savory soups. Enjoy their most popular burger topped with Jack Daniels® BBQ sauce and served with beer-battered onion rings or fries. Or try their pit-smoked poultry, fish, ribs and steaks.

Diners enjoy traditional starters from cheesy quesadillas and Thai calamari, to nachos, wings, and spicy jalapeño beer fries and jalapeño cornbread. The Brewery offers a generous selection for vegetarians, serving savory Greek pasta, basil pesto linguine, hummus wrap, asiago & garlic cheese ravioli, burritos, enchiladas, burgers, and more.

Main entrees include pub burgers, pastas, sandwiches, wraps and salads. Their popular seafood dishes include beer-battered cod fish & chips and fish tacos, pastas made with blackened

tilapia, and fillets of Atlantic salmon and wahoo. Their signature Texas pit-smoked chicken, tri-tip, pork ribs, and combo platter are the hottest items on the menu, along with 10 ounce cuts of New York steak and slow-roasted prime rib.

Moab Brewery features a unique in-house gelato kitchen. The gelato cart showcases up to twenty delicious creams and sorbettos, many of them are original flavors created by their in-house gelato cooks. These smooth Italian gelatos are made from natural ingredients and have a local following as impressive as their beverage counterparts.

Moosejaw Pizza & Dells Brewing Company

The Pub

The locally owned and operated Moosejaw Pizza & Dells Brewing Co. is one of the largest brewpubs in the Midwest. The Canadian Northwood's themed brewpub has comfortable seating for over 500 guests. Family dining rooms are located on each floor along with three distinct bars, a large arcade and the open air microbrewery all within this 24,000 square feet rustic, tri-level restaurant, located in the heart of Wisconsin Dells. The central Wisconsin city known as "The Dells" is a popular Midwestern tourist destination, hosting an annual five million visitors each year to family fun at "The Waterpark Capital of the World".

Dells Brewing Co. produces up to 1,000 gallons of hand-crafted beer a day for guests to enjoy while dining or at any of the three bars located inside the brewpub. They even started to bottle their beers, so now you can take the flavor home from your vacation! The brewpub features 6 year-round beers on draft, along with 4 seasonal brews. Moosejaw serves homemade pizzas and freshly prepared comfort food along with its hand-crafted brews, in a warm and inviting lodge setting, with plenty of space and activities for guests of all ages.

Owners

Moosejaw Pizza & Dells Brewing Co. was co-founded in 2002, by partners: Mark and Kristen Schmitz, Jack and Mary Waterman, and Turk and Judy Waterman. Moose Jaw is a city located in south-central Saskatchewan, Canada, on the Moose Jaw River. During the early 1900s, as Europeans settled throughout North America, an extensive tunnel system was built underground for maintenance of the building heating systems. During the era of Prohibition in the U.S., the Moosejaw Brewing and Malting Company, operated from 1906 to 1936, was believed to be Al Capone's hub for liquor. Using the underground tunnel system and the Canadian Pacific Railroad, Al Capone and his rumrunners were able to successfully distill and ship liquor in large quantities to Chicago for distribution. In 1985, a truck fell through a street revealing the extensive underground network connecting hotels to the brewery and railroad depot. Today, the historic Tunnels of Moose Jaw offer tourists a unique glimpse back in history at the famous bootlegging years of the roaring

1920s. Owner Turk Waterman came up with the historic name for their new brewpub, after researching for names that fit the Northwood's theme. He stumbled upon the name Moose Jaw and once he read about the rich and tumultuous legacy of the city he was convinced.

ATMOSPHERE

This popular restaurant opened its doors in 2002, and has developed a loyal customer base with locals and vacationing tourists ever since. Moosejaw is tastefully decorated in locally crafted wood railings and furniture, with a grand two-way fireplace and walls adorned with big game mounts. The open air microbrewery,

a dining area and Bob's Brewery Bar are located on the upper level. Bob's Bar is named for their very own bartender, Bob Fichter, a former World War II Naval Pilot. The main floor houses several large family-style dining rooms, the main taproom bar, and a gift store called Little Buddy's Trading Post. The lower level, known as the Rathskellar, contains another dining area, spacious third bar complete with billiard table, dart board and televisions for premium sports viewing, and a state-of-the-art arcade and game room.

BEER AND SPIRITS

Dells Brewing Co., housed on the third floor of the restaurant, brews its hand-crafted beers, through a multi-step brewing and fermenting process using 15 copper-clad barrels. The brewpub serves 10 different styles of beer fresh from the tap, featuring the flagship beer and award-winning Rustic Red Ale, and the popular Honey Ale, both also now available in bottles. The other four year-round brews featured are the Golden Lager, Dells Pilsner, Raspberry Crème Ale, and the Kilbourn Hop Ale. The restaurant also rotates four seasonal beers on tap for guests to experience. Headliners include: a Wisconsin Wheat, a full-bodied Coffee Stout, and a traditional Blonde Bock. A special hand-crafted Apple Ale showcases fresh cider from the Kickapoo Orchard in Gays Mills, Wisconsin. They also brew Root Beer, Grape, and Orange

sodas on premise, both their hand-crafted beers & sodas may also be enjoyed at their sister restaurant, Buffalo Phil's Pizza & Grille.

Brewmaster, Jamie Baertsch holds the title as "Only Female Brewmaster in Wisconsin", recently perfected her recipes for bottling. Moosejaw beer aficionados can now pickup ½ gallon growlers, ¼ and ½ barrels, or a six-pack of their favorite craft beer for home enjoyment. Jamie is also a proud member of the Pink Boots Society, an organization of women that play key roles in the brewing industry and has been a featured speaker at the Craft Brewers Conference.

Beer connoisseurs have fun pairing the distinct ingredients and flavors of each featured beerwith an equally complimentary dish. Beer enthusiasts savor such flavor-minded combinations,

including: the Rustic Red with Chicken Fajita Specialty Pizza or the Oktoberfest with an Elk Burger. In Wisconsin, Friday Night Fish Fry is a rite of passage… wash it down with a Dells Pilsner and you are truly a Wisconsinite! Beers are served by the pint, pitcher, growler or try a sampler!

CUISINE

Moosejaw's menu provides diners with a large variety of food, including: Beer & Cheese Soup, Portabella Moose-shroom Melt, Mozzarella Sticks that are hand wrapped in wonton wrappers, and Moosejaw Beer Bread served hot with honey butter. The Beer Bread is so good it shows up on both the appetizer menu as well as the dessert menu!

While guests enjoy the dynamic duo of piping, hot pizzas *(with dough made fresh daily)* and one of those 10 handcrafted beers, they can feel good about the fact that the Moosejaw is a Travel Green Wisconsin business. The brewing equipment is on sensors to conserve energy, the used grains from the brewing process end up as

feed for a local riding stable, and the delivery vehicles – VW bugs nicknamed "Bio-Bugs" – are run on recycled kitchen oil.

Moosejaw also features a large selection of hearty dinner entrees, along with a build your own pasta dish option. Diners select their pasta, sauce, meat and an assortment of toppings and savor their custom creation with salad or soup, and breadstick. Dinner entrees include a Broiled Walleye, native to Canada and Wisconsin, Iowa Chops, New York Strip and Porterhouse. Pops' Old Fashioned Beer Ribs, named in homage to owner Mark Schmitz's father, Phil aka Pops, are a guest favorite.

Kudos to a restaurant that knows its younger clientele and names menu items: Bucksnort Burger, Chicken Antlers, Old Faithful *(a grilled cheese)* and the Mighty Minnow Friday Night Fish Fry. Plus they have paper moose antlers that top off your kids, both young & old!

Moosejaw desserts include a 24-Karat Carrot Cake, and a warm Bread Pudding made with the Moosejaw Beer Bread. Cheesecake, peanut butter pie, ice cream sundaes and handcrafted Root Beer floats ensure a perfect meal-ender for every palate.

PELICAN PUB & BREWERY

PELICAN
PUB & BREWERY

THE PUB

Welcome to the home of 'beer cuisine.' Here it is much more than just beer and food. It's about how those two life pleasures can work together to create something truly unique. The Pelican Pub & Brewery is the Northwest's only oceanfront brewery and has become a landmark for craft beer and food enthusiasts. Not only does the Pelican have an unobstructed view of Haystack Rock, but their beers have won countless national and international awards including DRAFT Magazine's Top 25 Beers of the World list in 2008, 2009 and 2010 for their Kiwanda Cream Ale and the Great American Beer Festival's prestigious "Brewpub of the Year" award, which the Pelican has won three times. They have also won "Champion Large Brewpub" at The World Beer Cup in 2008 and 2012.

OWNERS

In 1995, Jeff Schons and Mary Jones purchased an old brick building on the oceanfront in Pacific City, Oregon. Over Sunday morning coffee, Jeff and Mary came up with the idea of opening an oceanfront micro-brewery. As they knew almost nothing about the brewing process, they decided to attend a Craft Brewers conference in Portland, Oregon.

While at the conference it occurred to Mary that there might be a brewer in attendance that might be interested in joining the Pelican Pub & Brewery. On a hand-written 3x5 note card tacked to a bulletin board, Mary scribbled the details of what they were looking for.

It was this note card that caught Darron Welch's attention. After several eager phone calls to Jeff and Mary, Darron and his fiancé moved to Pacific City and Darron began brewing test batches of beer down the street in mini-storage units while the Pelican was under construction. On May 4, 1996, the Pelican opened its doors.

In 2004, a fellow named Ken Henson decided he wanted to find a friendly small town in the Northwest to raise his family. Happily, Ken is a top notch Chef *(not to mention all-around good-natured kind of guy)* and his advancement to General Manager of the Pelican Pub & Brewery has been a critical element in the ongoing efforts to bring together world class hospitality

and unique menu offerings to complement the outstanding handcrafted beers.

Over the years, Darron and Ken have both become partners in the Pelican Pub & Brewery and so there are now four owners, Jeff Schons, Mary Jones, Darron Welch and Ken Henson.

At the Pelican Pub & Brewery the atmosphere is laid back, but they take their beers very seriously. With six award-winning beers available on tap and bottled year-round, you'll never be disappointed. In addition, the Pelican makes it their mission to always have some extra

seasonal or one-off beers on tap to keep things interesting.

The Pelican brews on a copper-clad, steam fired, three-vessel, 15 bbl *(465 gallons)* system that was custom built for us by Pub Brewing Systems in Santa Rosa, California. The copper cladding is for decoration only, and no copper touches the beer at any step in the process. The kettle was built by Newlands Systems and installed in 2006. It features bottom and side jackets and an internal calandria.

The brewery is equipped with four 15 bbl

unitank fermenters, two 30 bbl unitank fermenters, four 15 bbl serving tanks, one 7 bbl *(217 gallons)* serving tank, and one 13 bbl serving tank. Most of the beers are filtered on a three-meter, horizontal leaf, Velo filter.

The Pelican Pub & Brewery core beer lineup includes Kiwanda Cream Ale, MacPelican's Scottish Style Ale, Doryman's Dark Ale *(which is considered their 'flagship' beer as it was the first brew made at the Pelican)*, India Pelican Ale and Tsunami Stout. In 2012, Silverspot IPA claimed a permanent slot in the Pelican lineup. A portion of the proceeds from the sale of this beer will help fund conservation efforts for the

Oregon Silverspot Butterfly. Drink a beer, save a butterfly…why not?

The Pelican also produces 12 seasonal beers throughout the year. The most popular seasonal beer being their highly anticipated and award-winning Mother of All Storms, a limited production Kentucky bourbon barrel-aged barleywine-style ale. Craft beer lovers eagerly await the official release date for this beer in November, which has been designated "Mother's Day".

Cuisine

The Pelican Pub & Brewery is open for

breakfast, lunch and dinner with a menu that boasts everything from a tower of onion rings to pale malt crusted salmon, there's definitely something for everyone. Dine in the casual atmosphere of the spectacular ocean view dining room or celebrate summer by enjoying your meal beach side on the patio.

Many guests ask us what we mean by 'beer cuisine.' Well, what is more important, the beer or the food? The Pelican says both. In fact, The Pelican Pub & Brewery is a world leader in the pairing of food and beer. After all, they've been doing it for 16 years. The executive chef and brewmaster make it their daily mission

to understand how food and beer flavors complement one another.

PORTNEUF VALLEY BREWING

THE PUB

Portneuf Valley Brewing *(PVB)* is located in the Historic Warehouse District in Pocatello, Idaho. It is five blocks west of Idaho State University and abuts the main Union Pacific Rail yard. Fifty years ago the building was the bottling plant for the adjacent East Idaho Brewing Company, which operated post-prohibition into the mid-1950s. Prior to prohibition Franklin and Hayes Brewing operated in another building on the same block, making PVB the third brewery in the area during the past century.

In 1996 PVB opened in a subleased space in a sports bar. Its sudden shutdown in 2002 forced operations to relocate. When owner Penny Nichols Pink acquired the current building in 1999, it was merely a junk filled husk with no utilities and a leaking roof. The building's only use in the prior ten years was as a haunted house.

After three years of gutting the space with her two teenage sons and many friends, Penny had to return to work to finance renovations and move the brewing operation.

PVB moved to its current location in June of 2002 and the evolution to become a full-fledged brewpub began. Most recently, PVB completed renovations of the 3,000 square foot loft. The Loft has a beautiful custom built bar, stage for live music, and room for catering large parties and various events.

OWNER

Brew mistress and owner Penny Pink was just a high school dropout fortunate enough to attend college. Penny worked much of her career as an analytical chemist and microbiologist. She worked about 20 years at the nearby Idaho National Laboratory, most recently doing environmental compliance managing radioactive hazardous waste.

Penny home brewed for 7 years prior to opening PVB. Her quest to find a way to leverage her background doing something closer to home spurred her to venture into starting a microbrewery. She states in her menu cover story, "I love to brew. I love to bake. I love fresh wholesome food. I decided to turn my love affair with yeast into a business and see what I could do to catalyze some cultural diversity in this neck of the woods."

Penny built her original brewing system in her

driveway out of scrap stainless steel tanks from a defunct soda pop factory. Since then she acquired a professional brewing system that allows her to create a variety of ales and lagers. She and her brewing staff keep eight regular beers on tap ranging from the very light Penny's Extra Pale Ale to the silky Midnight Satin Cream Stout. Every season sees new brewer's specials and seasonals with crazy new beers crafted for the yearly anniversary party.

Atmosphere

PVB is open to all ages for lunch and dinner Monday to Thursday, 11am-10pm and until midnight on Friday and Saturday. The atmosphere is warm, casual and relaxed. There is no smoking allowed inside and no televisions, encouraging people to interact with one another in a healthy environment. Over the years PVB has become more of a social hub for Pocatello than a pub. With live music four nights a week, parties, concerts, poetry readings, theater productions, science seminars, and fundraisers, there's always something fun going on.

Penny bootstrapped her way through four phases of renovation over the past decade. The brewpub has a small stage, bar, and views of the brewing operation near the entrance. The dining room to the rear features casual booths

and tables that can accommodate groups large or small on the main floor. A deck with outdoor seating is at the back with an ADA accessible ramp into the building. The view from the deck showcases the ever-changing array of graffiti laced trains in the rail yard with a backdrop of mountains surrounding the Portneuf Valley.

The spacious loft has capacity for 175 people. Large group parties happen regularly, served up with scrumptious buffet style meals. The rustic red brick walls and exposed beam work, reminiscent of its heritage as a warehouse, has been accented with wrought iron stairs and warm, knotty pine accents. The new bar

upstairs easily accommodates crowds to hear the bands on the weekends. There's room for dancing but also spaces tucked away far enough from the performers to hear the music and converse easily.

Beer and Spirits

PVB routinely has ten beers on tap at both bars, and occasionally a special brew in The Loft. A fun way to try all the beers is to share a sampler tray with friends. Beers on tap range in color from light to dark, like the Ligertown Lager, Twisted Stick Amber Ale, the award winning Belligerent Ass Nut Brown Ale, Grog IPA, and brewer's specials like the Scout Mountain

Espresso Stout. These beers are crafted to provide full pallet of hues and hoppy characteristics for a wide variety of taste preferences. PVB also brews the popular Carrie Nation Old Fashioned Sarsaparilla root beer. All are available to take home in half-gallon growlers.

PVB also has an extensive wine list. More than a dozen wines are available by the glass and 35 wines are available by the bottle. The variety of beverages is perfect for pairing wine and beer selections with the array of delicious food offered.

Cuisine

PVB provides an assortment of fresh, wholesome pub grub for lunch, dinner, and late night snacks. Everything on the menu is made to order, so while it takes longer especially on busy nights, it is well worth the wait.

Popular appetizers include the antipasto tray, spinach artichoke dip, giant salty pretzel, macho nachos with "green death" roasted jalapeño salsa, and more. Fresh soups made daily pair well with a wide variety of sandwiches, salads and fresh baked bread, including whole-wheat Ciabatta beer bread made with spent grain from the brewing process.

Entrées include burritos, pizza, pasta, lasagna, curry, jambalaya, teriyaki, and comfort food like the Wacky Mac-N-Cheese. Vegetarian options are available and fresh spinach can be substituted for rice or pasta on many dishes as a low-carb option.

Complete your experience with house-made New York style cheesecake, brownies, apple bars a la mode or a frothy Sarsaparilla root beer float.

PUBBELLY

THE PUB

Pubbelly is the first Asian-inspired Gastropub in the South Beach Miami scene, a trendy chef-driven neighborhood tavern catering to locals with inventive dishes and unique libations. Owners, Schreiner, Navarro, and Mendin not only found their niche in the eclectic high-low Sunset Harbour neighborhood, but in many ways redefined it with their successful launch of Pubbelly in 2010. Pubbelly's gastropub fare is unique, combining seasonal Asian ingredients with European cooking techniques to create bold American cuisine. Guests enjoy upscale Asian street food and haute cuisine of homemade pate, sausage and pork belly, duck and pork rillettes, specialty terrines, braised dishes and pickled vegetables. The evolving chef-driven menu is paired with a unique and well-sourced sake program, specialty sake cocktails, and a thoughtful beer and wine menu focused on craft breweries and boutique wine producers from the Americas, Asia and Europe. Many of the Pubbelly dishes are presented on small plates, perfect for sharing with friends in their warm pub atmosphere accompanied by daily music themes.

OWNERS

The Pubbelly restaurant was founded by three young entrepreneurs of deep Spanish heritage and training, complimenting strengths and skills, and a common passion for exceptional food, beverage and service. Andreas Schreiner, Pubbelly Founding Partner and Managing Director, grew up working in his upscale family restaurant in Puerto Rico. He obtained his Bachelors from Florida International University's Hospitality School, and a Masters in Business Administration from Nova Southeastern University. Schreiner spent the next 12 years in four countries, working his way up within the food and beverage management industry. In 2010, fluent in Spanish, English, German and Italian, and a certified sommelier, Schreiner returned to Miami to pursue a lifelong dream of owning his own restaurant.

Sergio Navarro, Pubbelly Founding Partner and Chief Designer, trained at his Basque mother's side, before pursuing his culinary arts degree from Spain's prestigious Hotel Escuela Comunidadde Madrid. Navarro honed his culinary and pastry techniques working in La Broche of Madrid, earning the restaurant two Michelin stars during his tenure. In 2001,

Navarro relocated to the United States to open La Broche of Miami, followed by high profile positions designing and creating vibrant international cuisine for Mundo, Nobu Miami, and Mercadito of Miami.

Pubbelly Founding Partner and Director of Culinary Operations, Jose Mendin also grew up in Puerto Rico, working with exotic ingredients in his great grandmother's busy kitchen, at an early age. After earning his Culinary Arts Degree from Johnson and Wales, Mendin spent the next decade working and training abroad, mastering his culinary trade at Nobu London and Michelin-rated El Chaflan in Madrid. Mendin

played an integral role in the opening of Nobu Miami, before serving as chef de cuisine for SUSHISAMBA, and then launching three new restaurants in Las Vegas, Chicago and Miami. After the successful debut of Mercadito in Midtown Miami in 2010 with Navarro, the two chefs joined forces with Schreiner to cultivate a restaurant of their own.

Andreas Schreiner, Sergio Navarro and Jose Mendin opened the doors to Pubbelly in November 2010. The culmination of three dreams became the first Asian gastropub in Miami, and an overnight success. The dedicated threesome responded by opening Pubbelly

Sushi next door in 2011, and Macchialina, an Italian Pubbelly, in 2012. A much anticipated steakhouse gastropub is in the works for 2013.

Atmosphere

The Pubbelly is located on 20th Street on the quieter end of South Beach, in a rustic brownstone with brick walls, high ceilings, an open kitchen, and indoor and outdoor patio seating. The casual Sunset Harbour location attracts business from two causeways and tons of surrounding residents, serving a clientele of 90% locals. Guests of the gastropub enjoy an intimate and relaxed dining experience, and warm, intuitive service.

Beer and Spirits

The Pubbelly beverage program is designed to compliment every aspect of the dining experience, featuring quality beer, wine, sake and specialty cocktail accompaniments that evolve regularly with the food menu. The beer list showcases small, independent and traditional, craft breweries from the Americas, Asia and Europe. Guests savor 20 extraordinary crafted lagers, ales, porters and more, that run the gamut in flavor. Beer connoisseurs enjoy a variety of domestic pours, including: Hazed & Infused *(dry hopped ale)*, Flying Dog IPA and Gonzo, and Victory Brewing Company's Golden Monkey Tripel crafted with Asian spices.

The evolving wine menu includes a diverse selection of 40 crisp and rich whites, sparkling wines, and light to full-bodied reds sold by the glass, or bottle. Each featured vineyard produces unique grapes from a quality wine region worthy of celebration. With a sommelier at the helm, wine enthusiasts savor spectacular glasses of highly-prized wines, like the Emilio Moro from Ribera del Duero, Spain, on a daily basis.

Pubbelly also features a unique sake program to compliment their Asian cuisine. Special designation sakes like Konteki from Junmai Daiginjo-shu are crafted from pure rice, and like their beer counterparts are classified as very special brews. Specialty cocktails showcase featured sakes, fresh juice and produce, including: The Pineapple Ginger, a Peach Caliente, La Guagua and the Passion Martini.

CUISINE

The Pubbelly cuisine reflects the creative collaboration of its three owners, their Spanish heritage, international culinary training, and appreciation for concepts that work. They beautifully blend gastropub cuisine with Asian street food, staying true to the ingredients to serve patrons rich, homemade Asian comfort food with a gourmet twist. Regular menu changes are based on the seasonal and fresh produce, seafood and meats available from their purveyors all over the world.

Pubbelly regularly features lighter fare in their raw bar of oysters and stone crab claws, along with breads, nuts, cheese and chorizo.

Dumplings are an Asian mainstay and Pubbelly features innovative variations like: duck and pumpkin, chorizo and scallion, and short rib and corn. Traditional noodle and rice dishes showcase Pubbelly's signature pork belly, with a touch of lemongrass and poached egg.

Pubbelly features 20 plates bursting with bold flavors, a contemporary flair, and ideal for sharing. Diners enjoy mouth-watering kimchee, short ribs and pork belly. Authentic seafood fare includes: Japanese Amberjack, Squid, Octopus a la Plancha, and Bay Scallops from Nantucket. Duck, Buffalo Style Sweetbreads, barbequed pork wings and a 21-ounce Cowboy Wagyu Steak rounds out the diverse and savory entrees, with sides of pickled vegetables, shaved onions, green beans and more.

RAILSTOP GASTROPUB

THE PUB

Established inside the Crowne Plaza in 2011, Railstop Gastropub is the newest neighborhood pub in Alexandria and the first gastropub in Old Town. Located along the Western bank of the Potomac River, Old Town is the oldest neighborhood in the city and a high-income suburb for Washington, D.C., located just six miles north. This eclectic area is home to 140,000 residents and features a concentration of high-rise town homes, luxury hotels, galleries, boutiques and historic landmarks, along with urban boulevards, bike paths and the riverwalk bustling with walking tours, runners and cyclists. The Crowne Plaza hosts a large number of government employees, associations, business travelers and tourists each year, while its new gastropub, fashioned as a train station depot, caters to a 50-50 split of hotel guests and local residents. Railstop Gastropub combines the charisma of a classic English tavern with upscale cuisine, artisan cocktails and draughts, and good old-fashioned pub fun. Railstop is a popular watering hole with residents, and a favorite stop for out-of-towners passing through the mid Atlantic.

ATMOSPHERE

Crowne Plaza sits along historic train tracks, providing the Gastropub with its theme as a depot or railstop. Old Town's first gastropub caters to travelers and its local urbanites who relish a high-quality pub within walking distance. The dining room and bar-top provides seating for 76 patrons, with picturesque views of the Potomac River. Unique flooring and lighting creates a warm inviting atmosphere, with train memorabilia and vintage posters celebrating 200 years of U.S. railway history throughout. Unique chalkboard quotes from the country's founding fathers, flat screen TVs, daily happy hour, and live entertainment add extra appeal to the memorable food and libations served.

BEER AND SPIRITS

Railstop features craft beers and signature cocktails, along with full spirits. Five draughts are poured fresh, highlighting Alexandria's pride in their regionally crafted beers, and include: the smooth Fordham Copperhead Ale brewed in Annapolis, MD; the crisp single-malt Hook & Ladder Golden Ale from Silver Springs, MD; and a rich, malt-forward Legend Brown Ale made with toasted nuts, coffee and molasses in Richmond. Craft bottled beers from Dover,

DE include Old Dominion's Lager and Oak Barrel Stout, along with the Flying Dog Road Dog Porter from Frederick, MD. Classic Sam Adams Boston Lager, Stella Artois Belgium and Guinness are also served.

Railstop headlines nine specialty train station cocktails with a following of their own. Bourbon lovers enjoy the popular Caboose made with Woodford Reserve Bourbon, and The No. 7 fashioned with bourbon, apple liqueur, dry vermouth, and orange and pomegranate juices. The Conductor blends gin, mint, blackberry brandy and lime juice for a smooth ride, while the Express Freight exhilarates riders with

tequila, blood orange syrup and lime juice. Derailed is a powerful punch made with vodka, banana rum, peach schnapps and pineapple juice. Chug Chug is an easy-to-drink cocktail of pomegranate liquor, orange vodka and sour mix. The Engineers Whistle is a light cocktail made with raspberry vodka, sour mix and crème de cassis. Coal Car features light rum, grapefruit juice and passion fruit puree, while the Boxcar elevates the martini with Remy Fine Cognac Champagne and a sugar rim. Spirits drinkers also enjoy classic Manhattans, Martinis, Cosmos, Mojitos and more.

CUISINE

The Gastropub offers distinctive pub food at the restaurant, and by way of hotel room service. The menu features creative starters, fresh soups and salads, and unique house-made burgers, sandwiches and entrees. Traditional bar nuts are elevated to a savory selection of pickled finger foods, as drinkers nibble on olives and cocktail onions in a zesty citrus marinade, or smoked salmon deviled eggs with capers, red onions and tomatoes. Fried pickles are a favorite snack with regulars, along with deep fried ham and cheddar bites, bruschetta and garlic hummus.

Starters include herbed polenta with ratatouille,

lamb kofta with cucumber mint sauce, and the signature house-made spicy pork sausage served with sweet escovitche. A cup of homemade chicken and macaroni soup, or bowl of jumbo shrimp in a chardonnay, lobster and garlic broth are served piping hot with herbed croutons. Fresh spinach, Caesar and mesclun salads combine vegetables, cheeses, candied walnuts and house-made dressings to delight vegetarians.

Grilled portabella and freshly-ground Angus Beef burgers are served on a Challah bun with fries, tots or the signature fried potato salad. The Jerk provides a spicy Jamaican twist to the all-American burger, while pub sandwiches

are lifted with jumbo lump crab cakes, southern fried chicken, fried haddock and the house sausage.

Gourmet-styled mains include: NY Strip Steak Frites; Seafood Sausage of monkfish, scallops, shrimp and haddock; Pork Belly with gorgonzola polenta; and Vegetarian Strudel of wild mushrooms and goat cheese. Pan-seared stripped bass is featured every Monday, followed by a grilled pork lion on Tuesday, and roasted vegetable risotto every Wednesday. The Railstop features a blue cheese fillet mignon on Thursday, and Friday's favorite of Old Dominion lager-battered fish & chips. A pan-seared salmon is Saturday's headliner, followed by house-made meatloaf and garlic mashed potatoes on Sundays.

Four sweet treats include a signature Vanilla Bean Crème Brulee, along with Baked Chocolate Puddin' and Berry Cobbler, both served a la mode. A caramelized pineapple and ginger sauce highlights the traditional cheesecake as anything but ordinary.

SIMMZY'S

THE PUB

Simmzy's Pub of Manhattan Beach is a serendipitous gourmet burger joint and craft beer pub,– the perfect balance of artisan comfort food and libations - , with a relaxed beachside neighborhood appeal. Brothers, Mike and Chris Simms opened the doors to their new beachside gastropub in April 2009, stumbling happily into an untapped niche: upscale burgers and beer served in a flip-flop-friendly atmosphere. Three years later, they launched a second Simmzy's for the locals in Long Beach.

Guests of the pubs are mostly locals – dog-walkers, joggers, strollers, surfers and sunbathers - who enjoy sophisticated flavors in their intimate and casual beach community. Sandy and sunburned patrons enjoy savory burgers (*Simmzy's free-roaming Angus Beef, and Chef Anne's decadent house vegetarian-blend*), hot wood-fire grilled fish-tacos, gourmet salads of fresh shrimp, free-range chicken, avocados, apples and walnuts. This fresh, inventive gastropub fare is paired with unique regionally crafted ales, stouts, lagers, and red and white wines. The service is warm and inviting, unassuming and generous like the brothers. Simmzy's Mantra – "We make regulars one local at a time".

OWNERS

Brothers Mike and Chris Simms, both successful restaurant owners, founded Simmzy's Pubs. Mike Simms and his Culinary Partner, Anne Conness, opened Tin Roof Bistro in Manhattan Beach in 2009 as well, where they worked tirelessly on the perfect burger recipe, and began exploring the local craft breweries and vintners in their region.

Simmzy's is the result of an unlikely combination: homecoming and boredom. Chris Simms, the owner of 11 Lazy Dog Cafes, had just moved back to the neighborhood, living in close proximity for the first time since high school. Mike's passion for craft beers spilled over into his family garage, where he and Chris began home brewing. Their wives were less than thrilled by this development. So the brothers decided they needed a craft beer bar within walking distance. But the joint would also have to serve great food and wine so their spouses would occasionally join them. Unfortunately, such an establishment did not exist in Manhattan Beach.

Around this time, Chef Anne serendipitously mentioned to Mike, "I'm so bored, I would flip greasy burgers...at the beach." A week later, he asked her to meet him at 229 Manhattan Blvd., and pointed to a dilapidated little restaurant, "Here's your burger joint!" Simmzy's was born.

Atmosphere

Simmzy's Pubs are small, intimate, gourmet burger joints, catering to the local and pedestrian-friendly beach culture of Manhattan Beach and Long Beach. The building architecture is fashioned from an authentic lifeguard tower, using the same railings. The design purposely keeps the space open to the outside in order to make the most of Southern California's sunshine. Guests of the gastropubs enjoy this intimate and relaxed neighborhood atmosphere, while relishing extraordinary crafted food and libations.

Beer and Spirits

Simmzy's features a quality beer and wine menu consisting of unique, independent, craft breweries and vintners. The Simms brothers consciously partner with other local, small businesses committed to quality production. Each brewery and craft beer is diligently researched to delight guests with the hard-to-find, hand crafted ales, complex lagers, porters

and more - that they might otherwise never experience. Simmzy's pours 24 craft beers from tap, rotating new brews into the mix on a regular basis. Beer connoisseurs enjoy diverse flights and off the handle pours, savoring their way through local craft breweries on California's coast.

Simmzy's showcases Strand craft beers, always featuring one on tap draft, with specialty drafts introduced throughout the year. Two friends opened Strand Brewing Company in 2009, in a down economy. Their 24th Street Pale Ale and Beach House Amber proved to be a hit with the beach culture as a perfect accompaniment to the Simmzy's Burger. Other current features include

Deschutes Obsidian Stout, Chimay Trippel, Dogfish Head, and Rogue Hazelnut Brown.

Mike Simms worked in Napa Valley, and also maintains a well-sourced, evolving menu of reds and whites by the glass for Simmzy's grape drinkers. The wine list features carefully selected, small production vintners that produce a unique experience, continuing the brother's commitment to hand crafted products. Wine enthusiasts savor 3- and 6-ounce pours of Chappellet Cabernet or Chardonnay from Au Bon Climat, Stolpman Syrah from Santa Barbara, and Sauvignon Blanc produced by Craggy Range. Special reserve wines are featured daily.

CUISINE

Simmzy's cuisine is the culmination of two brothers, the marriage of their passions for great burgers and craft beers, and a classically trained chef. Simms Culinary Partner Anne Conness applies sophisticated techniques to produce casual handcrafted cuisine for the Tin Roof Bistro and Simmzy's Pubs. The Simms and Chef Anne are committed to sourcing local, responsibly-grown, seasonal ingredients for the food they serve, currently showcasing Tanimura & Antle Artisan Lettuces, Breadbar Breads in El Segundo, and the Drake Family Farms Goat Cheese. The Pub serves a small variety of high-quality gourmet burgers, hot sandwiches, and California pub fare, keeping the food menu simple, yet memorable.

Simmzy's famous burgers are made with Midwest farm-raised Angus cattle, a wood-fire grilled house lamb patty, and special vegetarian patties of a quinoa, faro and tofu blend. Delicious hoagies and panini are made with wood-fire grilled salmon and free-range chicken breasts, slow-cooked spice and vinegar pulled pork, and local artisan goat cheese. Fresh accompaniments include homemade pesto and garlic aioli, Simmzy's chow chow onions, candied bacon, apple slaw and avocado puree.

Diners enjoy a side of hot shoestring fries, traditional and sweet, with blue cheese drizzle. Guests with lighter palates can choose from fresh inventive salads, soups and starters. Salads include a savory Chicken, Apple & Walnut, a

Cabo Ahi, and Shrimp, Citrus & Avocado, with starters like the fresh Ahi Tartar and Sun-Dried Tomato Hummus. Traditional pub fare includes a house recipe for 15-Minute Wings, a generous Chili Verde Nachos, and Grilled Fish Tacos of wild-caught Oregon Rock Cod.

Simmzy's Pub features special weekend brunch plates of hearty breakfast favorites made from cage-free organic eggs, served with a special house Peach Sangria. A Kid's Menu is offered for younger patrons of small burgers, grilled cheese and chicken tenders. Homemade desserts include creative interpretations of American favorites: Chocolate S'mores Pudding, and Apple Filled Donuts.

Skagit River Brewing Company

The Pub

Skagit River Brewing Co. is one of Washington's best microbreweries and BBQ joints, serving residents and tourists, unforgettable big hops and Northwest pub grub for the past 20 years. Mt. Vernon is the county seat for Skagit County, with a long-time reputation as one of the "Best Small Cities in America". Traveling 150 miles from its origin in British Columbia, Skagit River winds it way south to Mt. Vernon, connecting the endearing city of tulips and pristine farmlands with fly-fishers and nature lovers from all over. Skagit River Brewing Co. was founded on the idea that quality house-brewed beers and sodas should be accessible to everyone. Tapping into the phenomenal resources surrounding them, the brewery sources Yakima Valley hops, northwest grown barley and wheat,

and pure waters to produce award-winning ales, lagers, stouts and signature Root Beer. A complimenting menu of high-quality pub favorites includes Wood-smoked BBQ ribs and wings, half pound burgers, made-from-scratch pizzas, and homemade s'mores. Comfortable indoor and outdoor dining, lounging sofas, and live music add extra ambience to the small home feel of the Skagit River Brewing Co. and its big hops.

Owners

Charlie Sullivan founded Skagit River Brewing Co. in 1993, to provide residents with a pub house of their own, serving high-quality food and house brews made local by supporting local farmers. Eric Lint joined Sullivan's team in 1997, as manager of the brewery and restaurant operations, and in 2008, stepped into his current role as President and CEO. Lint maintains the high standards his guests and local farmers have come to cherish. A native to Washington, Lint attended school in Burlington, and studied accounting at Western Washington University. Much of Lint's success can be attributed to his deep roots in the community and long tenure with the brewpub, along with his philosophy, "do what you love well, and the money will follow".

Atmosphere

With a widespread reputation for outstanding brews and the best BBQ in town, Skagit River Brewing Co. has been a central hub for Mt. Vernon residents for two decades, and a

destination location for many visitors to the area renowned for its fly-fishing adventures. Skagit River is one of the last unspoiled rivers in North America, still home to all five species of migrating Salmon, and two types of trout, welcoming fly fishers from all over the world to unique experiences with nature. The Skagit River, historic railway and Interstate-5 provide convenient access to downtown Mt. Vernon, established in 1889. The charming city features an eclectic mix of historic homes and buildings, revitalized theatres, galleries, open markets and shops, and a picturesque riverwalk alive with runners and bicyclists. Skagit River Brewing Co. is housed in a former produce warehouse on Third Street, in the heart of the downtown district. The massive rustic building is adorned in red brick and wood, with the look and feel of a saloon from the past. The large brewery, a proper tavern bar and family-styled dining room welcomes families and friends, and showcases live bands each week. An outdoor patio features large barbeque smokers and wooden picnic tables, and offers a unique ambiance of its own.

Beer

Skagit River Brewing Co. combines the finest local ingredients in Yakima Valley hops, Northwest grown barley and wheat, and pure water to handcraft its popular selection of brews,

sold and savored throughout Washington. The in-house brewery consists of a 20 barrel production facility with a renowned master brewer, complete with bottling in 22 ounce "bombers", sold local and shipped Sound Beverage And Odom Distributors. The brewery handcrafts eight year-round award-winning beers, along with seasonal productions from English ales to Russian Imperial stouts. Year-round headliners include: Skagit Brown Ale *(formerly "Steelie Brown")*, a popular brown ale known for its luscious roasted caramel and molasses flavors and smooth finish, and the perfect pairing with a variety of foods and desserts. Del Rio Lager is an easy-to-drink, light and bright lager, with a floral hop aroma, dry malt flavor and crisp finish. The robust London-styled Highwater Porter blends a rich variety of malted barley with coffee and chocolate flavors, creating a smooth, dry-roasted finish of hop bitterness. Sculler's IPA is a dry and roasty version of the old-world IPA, generously full of Northern Brewer hops and fruity malts, creating its unique aroma, flavor and drink-ability. Delrio Lager is an ultra-premium American lager, light-bodied with a nice balance of pilsner and honey malts, and crisp citrus flavor. This quality craft beer only contains three calories more than its big brand counterpart, Bud Light. Other notable concoctions include Skagit River's Farm

to Market Ale *(an English style bitter)*, created in support of the family farmers in the fertile Skagit River Valley. With every bottle sold, $.25 is donated to PCC Farmland Trust for local farm preservation.

CUISINE

A Northwest pub food menu of signature scratch recipes made with local sourced ingredients compliments the house-brewed suds. Classic pub starters include: artichoke dip, hummus, crab puffs, Mt. Baker Nachos and wood-fired quesadillas. A home-styled chicken pie, shepherd's pie, and bangers & mash are among favorite platters, along with a hearty burrito bowl.

The famous barbeque smokers and wood-fire grills yield melt-in-your-mouth beef brisket, St. Louis slow-roasted pork ribs, pulled pork, beer-simmered bratwurst, and unforgettable brewhouse wings. An assortment of savory wood-fire burgers are featured, including a

flavorful garden patty for vegans. The 9 inch wood-fire pizzas are made-from-scratch and baked to perfection on order. Inventive flatbreads include: Padilla Bay topped with Proscuitto, rosemary and feta, the Big River Barbeque, and Farmer's Market made with fresh artichokes, roasted red peppers and onions.

Seafood lovers dine on Cod Fish Tacos, Dungeness Crab Cakes, Oysters, wild-caught Coho Salmon, and Clams & Mussels in lemon and white wine sauce. A variety of soups, salads and pastas are also served, along with traditional wood-fire s'mores and ice cream floats showcasing the house Root Beer.

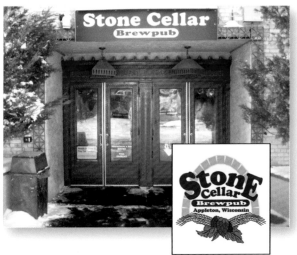

THE PUB

Stone Cellar Brewpub is home of the oldest operating brewpub in Wisconsin, and Appleton's beloved community Beer Garden. This historic brewery handcrafts 34 beers annually poured fresh in 150+ establishments throughout Northeast Wisconsin under the trademark name Stone Arch Brew House. Stone Cellar Brewpub serves natural, locally-sourced ingredients in their fresh gastropub cuisine, seven days a week, along with their signature beers and gourmet sodas. Owners Tom and Steve Lonsway and their team are passionate about making their food, their beer, their community, and the lives of their patrons better with a commitment to quality everything. Leading the charge towards a sustainable community, Stone Cellar Brewpub purveys organic fruits and vegetables, hormone and steroid-free dairy, and all-natural poultry, beef, pork and elk from other Wisconsin business

owners with certified humane practices. The brewery combines tradition and sustainability to provide locals and their guests with a taste of Wisconsin's best, in a warm, friendly pub of their own.

OWNERS

Stone Cellar Brewpub has a long history, dating back to 1858, when German immigrant, Anton Fischer settled in the budding puritan town, and along with the Fox River canal system, he built the first brewery operation in Outagamie County. Despite being a conservative city, Appleton residents embraced their brewery and began their long love affair with beer. In 1860, Fischer sold the brewery to Carl Muench, a foreman from the Joseph Schlitz Brewing Co. in Milwaukee. During his legacy, Muench added the outdoor beer garden that would come to be known as an Appleton institution.

The business was sold to the George Walter Brewing Co. in 1918, closing temporarily during the prohibition era. George Walter introduced Adler Brau that became the area's most popular beer until 1974, when the brewery closed its doors, no longer able to compete with national breweries. The building was remodeled to become the "Between the Locks" mall. In 1989, Appleton's Adler Brau beer was resurrected and put back into production under new ownership. The Adler Brau Brewery became Wisconsin's third brewpub. The oldest two have since closed their doors.

In 2004, father and son partners, Tom and Steve Lonsway acquired the brewpub and started their sustainable business initiative. Waste was reduced by almost 80%, as spent grains were sent to feed livestock on local farms, a composting program was implemented and the older inefficient appliances replaced. In 2012, the brewery was expanded with twice the building space, production was tripled and the craft beer line renamed Stone Arch Handcrafted Beers.

ATMOSPHERE

Stone Cellar Brewpub resides in the massive "Between the Locks" building. The brewery operation includes a 25-seat Tap Room for special tastings and events. The main bar is located in the cellar, encased in 158-year-old, thick stone walls and a dark, warm, old-style tavern ambience. The cellar level dining room includes the Carriage Room, and ample accommodations for families, dates, and groups. The English Room is an event room used for Beer School, Beer vs. Wine, Beer Dinners and available for private parties or business meetings. The famous Beer Garden is located outside along the west side of the building. Open May through September, the European-styled vine-wrapped brick cove features live music during the week, and remains one of Appleton's favorite watering holes for a cold beer or a tasty lunch in the summer.

Beer and Spirits

Wisconsin's oldest brewpub produces an annual 2,500 barrels of 34 handcrafted signature, specialty and seasonal ales for locals in Appleton and Northeast Wisconsin. Stone Arch Beer is poured fresh at 150+ establishments in the Fox Cities area, serving as far north as Eagle River, with a good deal of distribution as far south as Sheboygan. The active Mug Club of beer-loving cellar-dwellers is 500 members strong and growing.

Stone Arch Houdini Honey Wheat is an American style wheat beer made with layers of pure Wisconsin honey. Served in a weizen glass and garnished with an orange, this refreshing unfiltered brew is recommended with the organic beirgarten salad, and fish. Marquette Pilsner is characterized by a slightly dry, subtle and noble hop palate, commonly served in a pilsner glass alongside the brewhouse chicken

sandwich and baked haddock. The English Six Grain Ale is Tom Lonsway's own homebrew recipe. Brewed with barley, wheat, corn, oats, rye and rice, this easy-drinking English ale has a complex malt profile and nice hop balance, pairing nicely with the beer braised pot roast and elk burger. The Pie Eyed I.P.A. accents its huge hop flavors and flowery sharpness with a smooth finish, perfect with spicy entrees. The Scottish Ale is a caramel sweet beer with a malty profile and hints of smokiness, and the beer of choice with pizzas and burgers. The Stone Cellar Stout is a traditional oatmeal stout with moderate bitterness that rounds out smooth with the shepard's pie. Vanishing Vanilla Stout is a sweet English-style beer made with high-grade vanilla and is the perfect dessert beer.

Cuisine

Stone Cellar Brewpub features a large and well-rounded menu offering of traditional pub

cuisine made with fresh, organic and healthy ingredients, incorporating and paired with its craft beverages. Patrons enjoy a variety of starters, soups, burgers, pizzas, grilled entrees, pastas and pub favorites. The Fox Valley's only organic salad and soup bar, a kid's menu including craft sodas made on site, and an extensive gluten-free menu are provided to satisfy all palates.

Wisconsin farmers provide most of the ingredients used in the gastropub fare served. Elk and bison served in burgers and entrees are supplied through Navarino Valley Ranch, the pork, chicken and duck from Pinnacle Pastures, and certified grass fed beef burgers, sirloins and ribeyes from Black Earth Farms. Curds, breads and flights are made with artisan cheeses from Carr Valley, Marieke, Hooks, Sartori, Grande, Roth Kase, Edelweiss Creamery, Grass Point, Red Barn Dairy and Le Claire Farms. Other local partners include Gourmet Delight, Park

Ridge Organics, Keune's Authentic Produce Farm, and Briess Malting Company.

Pub favorites include traditional shepherd's pie, fish & chips, and Indian curry. A bison stroganoff, beer-braised pot roast, and jaeger schnitzel satisfy meat-lovers, while baked haddock, beer-battered walleye, ale-fried shrimp and a Friday fish fry of fresh lake perch wows seafood-lovers. Salad options are abundant for those who seek healthier choices.

THE PUB

The Three Rivers Brewery Block is a vast facility. It includes the brewery, pub, restaurant, pizzeria, Banquet/Meeting room and the tap and game room. It is all located in historic downtown Farmington, New Mexico. The restaurant and brewery was established in 1997 by John Silva and Bob and Cindy Beckley. Three Rivers Brewery is housed in the Andrews building built in 1912. This vintage building that has now been restored was home to Farmington Drug and the Farmington Times Hustler Newspaper and has many of the original antiquities still on display. Shortly after opening the brewery and restaurant, the were so successful that expansion was needed and the acquisition of buildings down the block slowly started one at a time. The building right next door was bought and turned into a dining room and an outdoor patio. The dining room is decorated with one of the largest beer label

collections in the world.

THE ATMOSPHERE

Lots of recreational pursuits and great fun for the family with a juke box, arcade games, pinball and two big screens TV's; one for the kids and one for the adults. Check out the entire wall of Italian themed graffiti spray can art done by one of their beloved employees "Kiko".

Next in the Brewery Block are the banquet, party, meeting, and etc. room where just about anything goes. A full two thousand square feet of private space set up with an entire audio visual system and three big screens.

Last but certainly not least is the Tap and Game room housed in two historic buildings that are now combined. The Tap and Game Room is the perfect place to have a couple of our 12 beers and play a game of pool, shuffleboard, darts, foosball , or just chill out and relax at the bar or the outdoor patio. This is where a lot of the locals like hanging out.

THE BEER

The brewery is a 10 BBl Pub system. They take advantage of all three stories and let gravity help move the beer along its way. The grain and mill are upstairs, the brewhouse and six fermenters are on the main floor and 14 serving tanks are down in the basement. With 12 of their own taps on at each location they make over 40 different beer styles in a year, all of which are sold on the Brewery Block. Their signature beer

is Papa Bears Golden Honey which is made with 60 pounds of local honey. And they have everything from light to dark, malty to hoppy, fresh fruit beers and cider. There is even an extreme beer, called X-Beer. Small fresh batches and many different styles has been their key to success. Over in the Tap and Game Room you can see a collection of accolades their beers have won over the years.

The Cuisine

The restaurant and pub with its classic historic ambience makes everything from scratch daily just like the brewery. In fact, everything they do is classic old school just like the buildings.

And you won't find any kind of franchise feel here. Everything is served fresh, including soups *(made from stocks)* salads, sandwiches, grilled brats, chicken, or build your own burgers, steaks ,ribs, seafood, and fish n chips, and homemade desserts. There is always a special everyday as well.

Go next door and step into the brick oven pizzeria where you will find hand crafted gourmet brick oven pizzas. Their proprietary dough and yeast sets them apart; they have our own live proprietary yeast strain that they cultivate and propagate daily using their papa bears golden honey beer.

So whatever you're in the mood for go on down to the Three Rivers Brewery Block and they will have something that will interest you. From the stories of their local ghost to the plethora of paraphernalia on the walls. There is always good beer, good food and good company.

TREMONT TAPHOUSE

THE PUB

Tremont Taphouse is Cleveland's first gastropub, located in the historic district of Tremont. Established in 1836, Tremont is listed on the National Register of Historic Places as one of the oldest neighborhoods in the city. Since the 1990s, the west side neighborhood has evolved into a hub for Cleveland's growing art community. There has been a large influx of young professionals, empty nesters, artists, musicians and hipsters. They are setting up shop in old factories repurposed to upscale lofts, restored Victorian homes and modern new construction. The pedestrian-friendly streets are lined with art galleries, boutique shops, and trendy restaurants and bars. The historic neighborhood also hosts farmers markets, art walks, performing art shows and several culinary inspired events. This Southside neighborhood of Cleveland is centrally located and is accessible via

Interstates 90, 490, 77, and 71. The gastropub sits at the heart of revitalized Tremont, west of the Cuyahoga River and south of the downtown business district, with easy access and appeal to Cleveland's 400,000 residents.

The London-influenced Beer Bar & Eatery is a casual pub house with a broad selection of 100 beers handcrafted in North America and Europe. A dedicated culinary team procures fresh, high quality, locally sourced ingredients to create their upscale yet approachable cuisine full of gastrological delights; from starters too good not to share, to desserts so good they're hard to share. Foodies enjoy dinner or "Cleveland's Best Brunch" in any of the distinct settings offered by The Taphouse. The bustling tavern atmosphere of the first floor is great for socializing. The second level offers an open kitchen that is center stage to contemporary dining room and cozy lounge. The dining room allows you to observe the heat of the culinary operations while not getting burned. The secluded lounge is ideal for intimate gatherings of friends and family. In summer time, the patio is a favorite inner city refuge. Adorned with a landscape that includes a fresh herb garden, lively perennials and a stone walled fire-pit is sublime and delivers the perfect backdrop of the city skyline.

OWNERS

Owners Jason Workman and Chris Lieb worked determinedly with their construction partner Jeff Leonard for 2 years renovating the hundred-year-old building into Cleveland's first gastropub. A

structure that included the old "Brothers Bar" and "Trinkas Café" provided 70 years of libations to generations of the cities blue collar steel and iron workers. As with many Midwestern cities, the steel industry has faded away. Along with the industry, gone are many of the traditional blue-collar workers that once populated this immigrant neighborhood. Today, Tremont's blue-collar factory and steel workers have been replaced with modern day blue-collar laborers, such as artists, hospitality staff, medical workers, and small business owners. The partners saw an opportunity in the deteriorating space and joined in with Tremont's Storefront Renovation initiative to begin restoring and renovating the historic building. The inspired team brought in a classically trained chef to create a food menu that not only superseded the expectations of a tavern atmosphere, but also challenged the most formal and upscale restaurants in both technique and flavor. Moreover, they diligently and exhaustively sourced a menu of handcrafted ales and lagers from the best brewers and breweries in the world.

Named for its historic neighborhood and selection of artisan beers, Workman and Lieb opened the doors to their Tremont Taphouse on Halloween night in 2007. Successfully tapping into the latest food trend of casual sophistication from across the ditch, Tremont Taphouse has become one of Cleveland's favorite watering holes and hip eateries. The gastropub has also gained the respect of many of the nations top brewers as one of the best beer bars in America. Ultimately, the owners wanted a place that represents and reflects the artistry and craft of food and beer… and a place that still manages to be a lot of fun.

ATMOSPHERE

Tremont Taphouse is fashioned in a 19th-century British-styled Italianate structure with a welcoming and comfortable ambience. The colorful building's interior is a blend of contemporary and industrial design with exposed brick walls, weathered oak floors and bright colored chalkboards representing the endless styles of beer. Alongside the bar are booths with tabletops crafted by local artists, each one unique and intriguing. Patrons enjoy the dynamic culinary team at work in the open kitchen, or their favorite Cleveland team on one of the HD televisions at the adjoining 40-foot concrete bar. On warm days the bar opens up its interior wall to create an indoor-outdoor atmosphere to the adjacent 2,000-square-foot outdoor patio. The upstairs offers an intimate lounge and a private dining room for parties. The Tremont Taphouse also hosts several events throughout the year, including Oktoberfest, A Winter Beer Fest & Outdoor Challenge, Running with the Santa's and a Belgian Beer Brunch. They also cater to visitors during the monthly art walk, the "Taste of Tremont"

food festival, and the Greek, Polish and other cultural festivals held throughout each year. The Taphouse is a destination location for Tremont urbanites, Ohio residents and visitors alike.

BEER

Cleveland's first gastropub features a distinctive beer bar with an unrivaled selection of more then 100 craft beers from around the world. Workman and Lieb celebrate the artistry and style of each beer by serving them in proper glassware fresh from a state of the art tap system that maintains and monitors proper temperature and pressure.

The beer bar features 48 beers on tap, rotating in new crafts each week. Artisan draughts from the Americas include Ohio favorites, Fathead's Head Hunter IPA and Hoppin Frog "Borris The Crusher," as well as regional offerings from Dogfish Head Squall from Delaware, Heavy Seas Below Decks from Maryland, Avery Maharaja from Colorado, The Bruery Mischief from California and Jolly Pumpkin La Parcela from Michigan. The list is also composed of many traditional European classics such as Germany's Reissdorf Kolsch and the Czech's flowery Staropramen, along with Belgium's Chimay White Cap, Delirium Tremens, Wayan Sour Saison, Rodenbach Grand Cru and Chouffe Biere du Soleil.

Daily hoppy hours, Monday Night Movies *(complete with gourmet popcorn)*, Tuesday Yappy Hour *(bring your dog to the patio)* and monthly

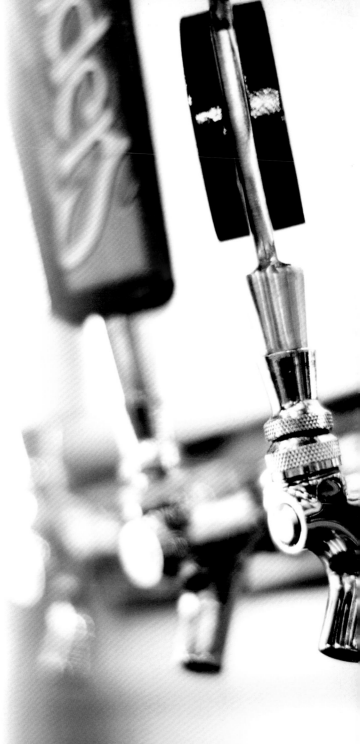

Beer & Food driven events provide aficionados with countless opportunities to taste their way around the globe each week.

Cuisine

While few pubs can rival Tremont's beer menu, the world-class dinner and brunch offerings prove The Tremont Taphouse is more gastropub than tavern. A culinary team headed by Chef Andrew Gorski, a graduate of the Culinary Institute of America who has studied under world class Chefs Thomas Keller and Alain Ducasse, procures fresh and exotic ingredients to create contemporary starters, soups and salads, extraordinary burgers and pizza and ambitious mains ranging from stout-braised short ribs to a Hungarian-inspired chicken paprikash.

The guests experience the latest dining trend sharing Small Plates of Pork Pate with pickled onions, Fried Gouda with a cranberry and onion marmalade, and savory Perogies traditionally stuffed with potato and cheese. Seafood delicacies include Moule Frites in a blue cheese and bacon broth, a sweet and fiery Calamari with cherry peppers and Sea Scallops with a Satsuma curd & petite kale. Tacos filled with house made Chorizo & Goat Cheese or Beef Tongue & Oysters are addicting. Unique Pizzas, baked in a 900-degree hearth deck oven produce the prefect crust and include components such as house made Pastrami and Arugula, Chorizo and Smoked Cheddar, or Wild Mushrooms adorned with White Truffle Oil.

The gastropub elevates the salad with Confit of Duck Leg and Tagliatelle Pasta with lamb, enoki and parsnips. Gourmet Burgers are house blend and ground with local pastured beef and explode with flavors from Artisan cheese, house cured and smoked bacon, candied onions and crispy shallots. The House Plates include a seared Duck Breast with preserved rhubarb and roasted cauliflower, seared Salmon with cranberry beans, and mouth-watering House Aged Rib-Eye dressed with shallots and blue cheese butter.

In visiting this gastro-pub, you may find the menu has changed, as it does with every season, but one assurance is The Tremont Taphouse will produce a memorable gastronomic experience.

Urge American Gastropub

The Pub

Urge American Gastropub is located in Rancho Bernardo, a quaint, family-oriented north county suburb of San Diego, California. Rancho Bernardo is home to 45,000 residents, three venerable golf courses, and a host of Fortune 500 corporations and small businesses alike. Urge is an American interpretation of the traditional English pub with a contemporary, and upscale twist. Owners Grant Tondro, Zak Higson, and Nate Higson offer fresh, hand-crafted pub fare along with an always-sophisticated tap list of fifty-one draught beers and an immense selection of bottled beers. Committed to a new rendition of classic American pub and bar food, the owners include the best hand-raised products to cultivate a casual yet sophisticated farm-to-table inspired menu. To accompany their ever evolving menu and house favorites, Urge offers the most delicious and sought-after craft beers in all of San Diego.

Owners

Restaurateurs Grant Tondro, Zak Higson, and Nate Higson also own 'The Barrel Room,' a vintage Wine Bar & Bistro and 'Brothers' Provisions,' an artisan cheese, charcuterie, wine and beer shop all located in Rancho Bernardo. A seemingly overnight sensation and known for its inviting atmosphere and dedicated wine list, the success of The Barrel Room naturally led to the opening of Urge American Gastropub just a few steps away. Having satisfied the local need for a welcoming wine bar, the owners wanted to create another genuine and honest experience for San Diego's emerging craft beer scene.

Born into a family of restaurant owners and educated at Rancho Bernardo High School, Grant Tondro became business partners with his longtime best friend Zak Higson and his brother Nate Higson when all were in their mid-twenties. After obtaining both his bachelor's degree in Business from San Diego State University and an MBA from University of Phoenix, Grant spent ten years working in the beverage industry. Zak Higson formally spent years in the wine industry while furthering his business knowledge as a controller for a large security company. Nate Higson also brings years of experience in the restaurant industry, having worked for several years as a manager at another local restaurant and supervising large-scale catering gigs for innumerable special events. Today, Grant serves as General Manager at Urge

Gastropub, Nate serves as the general manager at the Barrel Room, and Zak serves as general manager at Brothers' Provisions. Together, the three 'brothers' closely run each of their businesses and hope to further serve and enliven the community to which they owe their success.

Atmosphere

Urge American Gastropub has the feel of a modern speakeasy. Tucked behind the Barrel Room and other strip mall businesses, the five-thousand square foot gastropub includes a large patio, dining room, bar, and an intimate private room perfect for parties, meetings, and get-togethers. Though Rancho Bernardo is a quiet

San Diego community, Urge Gastropub host's large crowds of diverse professionals, families, and beer aficionados from all around San Diego and the west coast. The bar is the heart of the restaurant, featuring fifty-one rotating taps, high-definition flat screen TVs, and original artwork by local artists. Ultimately, Urge has a relaxed, warm, and down-to-earth atmosphere with an unpretentious vibe welcoming all food and beer lovers. They are proud to offer some of the best beer-centric events in town, with several award winning 'total-tap-takeovers,' high end private food and beer pairing dinners, and many single-brewery showcases during the weekdays. Some of the most eclectic and inspired tap lists

on the west coast can be found on any given day at Urge.

BEER

Urge prides itself on serving some of the most diverse, complex, and celebrated American and European craft beers. Inspired by San Diego's prestigious (and by some accounts, largest) craft beer scene, Urge maintains a high standard of service with its Cicerone® Certified Beer-Server staff. Urge has also developed many close relationships with some of the best breweries in town, often focusing its selections on rare, hard-to-get beers while filling its tap list to every taste and style guests could ask for. Many of the

most celebrated craft beer industry players call Urge one of their local hangouts and because of this, Urge has hosted some of the most exclusive events in San Diego. San Diego Beer Week, the annual celebration of all-things craft beer in San Diego, inspired Urge to host consecutive daily events that continued to impress for over a week. 'Blackout,' a beer event featuring all dark beers, is held each January to keep guests warm during the winter days. During the summer, Urge has continued to celebrate its anniversary with a weekend-long bash of music, outdoor food, and many special beer selections.

CUISINE

At the helm of Urge Gastropub's kitchen is executive chef Marc Liautard. With over twenty-years of experience, chef Marc often infuses locally sourced vegetables and unique proteins with craft beer found on tap. The flagship menu items include any of the half-pound burgers, featuring rabbit, wild boar, veal, and certified Angus beef along with inventive sauces, garnishes, and satisfying side items. Besides the absolutely delicious burgers, you can also find a dozen starters to share or any of its English renditions such as Sheppard's pie, Fish and Chips, and varying sausages sourced from local artisan Sausage Meisters. You can also find vegetarian/vegan options, house made soups, and lighter fare. Each and every dessert is made by sous chef Kailina Cunningham and Urge strives toward making as much food in-house as possible.